ACKNOWLEDGMENT

The author wishes to thank the following periodicals for permission to reprint the articles in this book: *Life, The Detroit Athletic Club News, The New Yorker, Vanity Fair, College Humor* and *The Bell Syndicate.* Thanks are also due to John Held, Jr., for permission to use his elegant engravings and to Carol Goodner for suggesting the title to the book.

THE EARLY WORM

THE
EARLY WORM

by Robert Benchley

WITH ILLUSTRATIONS BY GLUYAS WILLIAMS

BLUE RIBBON BOOKS

GARDEN CITY, NEW YORK

CONTENTS

THE EARLY WORM

A TALK TO YOUNG MEN

Graduation Address on "The Decline of Sex"

TO you young men who only recently were graduated from our various institutions of learning (laughter), I would bring a message, a message of warning and yet, at the same time, a message of good cheer. Having been out in the world a whole month, it is high time that you learned something about the Facts of Life, something about how wonderfully Nature takes care of the thousand and one things which go to make up what some people jokingly call our "sex" life. I hardly know how to begin. Perhaps "Dear Harry" would be as good a way as any.

You all have doubtless seen, during your walks in the country, how the butterflies and bees carry pollen from one flower to another? It is very dull and you should be very glad that you are not a bee or a butterfly, for where the fun comes in *that* I can't see. However, they think that they are having a good time, which is all that is necessary, I suppose. Some day a bee is going to get hold of a real book on the subject, and from then on there will be

3

mighty little pollen-toting done or I don't know my bees.

Well, anyway, if you have noticed carefully how the bees carry pollen from one flower to another (and there is no reason why you should have noticed carefully as there is nothing to see), you will have wondered what connection there is between this process and that of animal reproduction. I may as well tell you right now that there is no connection at all, and so your whole morning of bee-stalking has been wasted.

We now come to the animal world. Or rather, first we come to One Hundred and Twenty-fifth Street, but you don't get off there. The animal world is next, and off you get. And what a sight meets your eyes! My, my! It just seems as if the whole world were topsy-turvy.

The next time you are at your grocer's buying gin, take a look at his eggs. They really are some hen's eggs, but they belong to the grocer now, as he has bought them and is entitled to sell them. So they really *are* his eggs, funny as it may sound to anyone who doesn't know. If you will look at these eggs, you will see that each one is *almost* round, but not *quite*. They are more of an "egg-shape." This may strike you as odd at first, until you learn that this is Nature's way of distinguishing eggs from large golf balls. You see, Mother Nature takes no chances. She used to, but she learned her lesson. And that is a lesson that all of you must learn as well. It is called Old Mother Nature's Lesson, and begins on page 145.

Now, these eggs have not always been like this. That stands to reason. They once had something to do with a hen or they wouldn't be called hen's eggs. If they are called duck's eggs, that means that they had something to do with a duck. Who can tell me what it means if they are called "ostrich's eggs"? . . . That's right.

But the egg is not the only thing that had something to do with a hen. Who knows what else there was? . . . That's right.

Now the rooster is an entirely different sort of bird from the hen. It is very proud and has a red crest on the top of his head. This red crest is put there by Nature so that the hen can see the rooster coming in a crowd and can hop into a taxi or make a previous engagement if she wants to. A favorite dodge of a lot of hens when they see the red crest of the rooster making in their direction across the barnyard is to work up a sick headache. One of the happiest and most contented roosters I ever saw was one who had had his red crest chewed off in a fight with a dog. He also wore sneakers.

But before we take up this phase of the question (for it is a question), let us go back to the fish kingdom. Fish are probably the worst example that you can find; in the first place, because they work under water, and in the second, because they don't know anything. You won't find one fish in a million that has enough sense to come in when it rains. They are just stupid, that's all, and nowhere is their stupidity more evident than in their sex life.

Take, for example, the carp. The carp is one of the least promising of all the fish. He has practically no forehead and brings nothing at all to a conversation. Now the mother carp is swimming around some fine spring day when suddenly she decides that it would be nice to have some children. So she makes out a deposit slip and deposits a couple million eggs on a rock (all this goes on *under* water, mind you, of all places). This done, she adjusts her hat, powders her nose, and swims away, a woman with a past.

It is not until all this is over and done with that papa enters the picture, and then only in an official capacity. Papa's job is very casual. He swims over the couple of million eggs and takes a chance that by sheer force of personality he can induce half a dozen of them to hatch out. The remainder either go to waste or are blacked up to represent caviar.

So you will see that the sex life of a fish is nothing much to brag about. It never would present a problem in a fish community as it does in ours. No committees ever have to be formed to regulate it, and about the only way in which a fish can go wrong is through drink or stealing. This makes a fish's life highly unattractive, you will agree, for, after a time, one would get very tired of drinking and stealing.

We have now covered the various agencies of Nature for populating the earth with the lesser forms of life. We have purposely omitted any reference to the reproduction of those unicellular organisms which reproduce by dividing themselves up into two, four, eight, etc., parts without any outside assistance at all. This method is too silly even to discuss.

We now come to colors. You all know that if you mix yellow with blue you get green. You also get green if you mix cherries and milk. (Just kidding. Don't pay any attention.) The derivation of one color from the mixture of two other colors is not generally considered a sexual phenomenon, but that is because the psychoanalysts haven't got around to it yet. By next season it won't be safe to admit that you like to paint, or you will be giving yourself

away as an inhibited old uncle-lover and debauchee.
The only thing that the sex-psychologists can't read
a sexual significance into is trap-shooting, and they
are working on that now.

All of which brings us to the point of wondering if
it *all* isn't a gigantic hoax. If the specialists fall
down on trap-shooting, they are going to begin to
doubt the whole structure which they have erected,
and before long there is going to be a reaction which
will take the form of an absolute negation of sex.
An Austrian scientist has already come out with the
announcement that there is no such thing as a hundred per cent male or a hundred per cent female.
If this is true, it is really a big step forward. It
is going to throw a lot of people out of work, but
think of the money that will be saved!

And so, young men, my message to you is this:
Think the thing over very carefully and examine the
evidence with fair-minded detachment. And if you
decide that, within the next ten years, sex is going
out of style, make your plans accordingly. Why not
be pioneers in the new movement?

THE SEED OF REVOLT

IN the hearts of many New Yorkers there glowed a strange and savage sense of satisfaction when fire, a few weeks ago, destroyed the wooden staging which had encased the lower half of the new Aeolian Building under construction at the corner of Fifth Avenue and Fifty-fourth Street. That fire may prove to be the torch igniting a citizens' revolt of city-wide proportions.

For several years now, ever since they began tearing down most of the buildings in New York and erecting others in their places to be torn down next year, pedestrians have been practically excluded from the use of their sidewalks. On each corner, and in the middle of each block, it has been necessary to tunnel through great wooden passageways, dodging avalanches of bricks on one side and workmen darting out from clammy recesses with wheelbarrows of mortar on the other. These workmen have a system whereby they lie in wait in the ground floor of the new building, each with a wheelbarrow full of unpleasant material poised ready, until you and I are directly upon the plank which slopes across the sidewalk to the waiting truck. Then, at

a signal from the boss, they charge out directly in
your path, shouting the Fascist war cry and scraping

They lie in wait in the ground floor of the new building.

the buttons off your waistcoat. At the same moment
a landslide of gravel is let loose from the fifth floor

crashing on top of the flimsy structure over your head and sending through a blinding shower of fine white powder which stirs up all that old catarrhal trouble which the doctor has assured you will cause your death one day.

If you evolve some maneuver calculated to evade this ordeal by going around the structure on the outside, you are confronted by a line of trucks backed up against the curb, making it necessary for you to go way out to the middle of the street, where you are immediately run over in the traffic.

For years now the supine citizens of New York have forgone the use of their sidewalks, having first been prohibited the use of their streets, until the fire in the new Aeolian Building chewed to pieces the wooden shanty and boardwalk and, it is to be hoped, did irreparable damage to dozens of wheelbarrows. It is said that the fire was caused by a workman leaving an acetylene torch burning in the basement. Whether it was really a workman or some nerve-racked patriot with the courage of his convictions does not matter now. The idea has been implanted in the minds of hundreds of citizens and it would not be surprising if, before autumn, construction companies had evolved some other way of erecting their buildings.

Sending through a blinding shower of fine white powder.

PAUL REVERE'S RIDE

How a Modest Go-Getter Did His Bit for the Juno Acid Bath Corporation

FOLLOWING are the salesman's report sheets sent into the home office in New York by Thaddeus Olin, agent for the Juno Acid Bath Corporation. Mr. Olin had the New England territory during the spring of 1775 and these report sheets are dated April 16, 17, 18, and 19, of that year.

April 16, 1775.
Boston.

Called on the following engravers this a. m.: Boston Engraving Co., E. H. Hosstetter, Theodore Platney, Paul Revere, Benjamin B. Ashley and Roger Durgin.

Boston Engraving Co. are all taken care of for their acid.

E. H. Hosstetter took three tins of acid No. 4 on trial and renewed his old order of 7 Queen-Biters.

Theodore Platney has gone out of business since my last trip.

Paul Revere was not in. The man in his shop

13

said that he was busy with some sort of local shin-dig. Said I might catch him in tomorrow morning.

The Benjamin Ashley people said they were satis-fied with their present product and contemplated no change.

Roger Durgin died last March.

Things are pretty quiet in Boston right now.

April 17.

Called on Boston Engraving people again to see if they might not want to try some Daisy No. 3. Mr. Lithgo was interested and said to come in to-morrow when Mr. Lithgo, Senior, would be there.

Paul Revere was not in. He had been in for a few minutes before the shop opened and had left word that he would be up at Sam Adams' in case anyone wanted him. Went up to the Adams place, but the girl there said that Mr. Revere and Mr. Adams had gone over to Mr. Dawes' place on Milk Street. Went to Dawes' place, but the man there said Dawes and Adams and Revere were in con-ference. There seems to be some sort of parade or something they are getting up, something to do with the opening of the new foot-bridge to Cambridge, I believe.

Things are pretty quiet here in Boston, except for the trade from the British fleet which is out in the harbour.

Spent the evening looking around in the coffee houses. Everyone here is cribbage-crazy. All they seem to think of is cribbage, cribbage, cribbage.

April 18.

To the Boston Engraving Company and saw Mr. Lithgo, Senior. He seemed interested in the Daisy No. 3 acid and said to drop in again later in the week.

Paul Revere was out. His assistant said that he knew that Mr. Revere was in need of a new batch of acid and had spoken to him about our Vulcan No. 2 and said he might try some. I would have to see Mr. Revere personally, he said, as Mr. Revere makes all purchases himself. He said that he thought I could catch him over at the Dawes' place.

Tried the Dawes' place but they said that he and Mr. Revere had gone over to the livery stable on State Street.

Went to the livery stable but Revere had gone. They said he had engaged a horse for tonight for some sort of entertainment he was taking part in. The hostler said he heard Mr. Revere say to Mr.

Dawes that they might as well go up to the North Church and see if everything was all set; so I gather it is a church entertainment.

Followed them up to the North Church, but there was nobody there except the caretaker, who said that he thought I could catch Mr. Revere over at Charlestown late that night. He described him to me so that I would know him and said that he probably would be on horseback. As it seemed to me to be pretty important that we land the Revere order for Vulcan No. 2, I figured out that whatever inconvenience it might cause me to go over to Charlestown or whatever added expense to the firm, would be justified.

Spent the afternoon visiting several printing establishments, but none of them do any engraving.

Things are pretty quiet here in Boston.

Went over to Charlestown after supper and hung around "The Bell in Hand" tavern looking for Mr. Revere. Met a man there who used to live in Peapack, N. J., and we got to talking about what a funny name for a town that was. Another man said that in Massachusetts there was actually a place called Podunk, up near Worcester. We had some very good cheese and talked over names of towns for a while. Then the second man, the one who knew about Podunk, said he had to go as he had a date with a man. After he had left I happened to bring the conversation around to the fact that I was waiting for a Mr. Paul Revere, and the first man told me that I had been talking to him for half an hour and that he had just gone.

I rushed out to the corner, but the man who keeps the watering-trough there said that someone answering Mr. Revere's description had just galloped off on a horse in the direction of Medford. Well, this just made me determined to land that order for Juno Acid Bath Corporation or die in the attempt. So I hired a horse at the Tavern stable and started off toward Medford.

Just before I hit Medford I saw a man standing out in his night-shirt in front of his house looking up the road. I asked him if he had seen anybody who looked like Mr. Revere. He seemed pretty sore and said that some crazy coot had just ridden by and knocked at his door and yelled something that he couldn't understand and that if he caught him he'd break his back. From his description of the horse I gathered that Mr. Revere was the man; so I galloped on.

A lot of people in Medford Town were up and standing in front of their houses, cursing like the one I had just seen. It seems that Mr. Revere had gone along the road-side, knocking on doors and yelling something which nobody understood, and then galloping on again.

"Some god-dam drunk," said one of the Medford-ites, and they all went back to bed.

I wasn't going to be cheated out of my order now, no matter what happened, and I don't think that Mr. Revere could have been drunk, because while he was with us at "The Bell in Hand," he had only four short ales. He had a lot of cheese, though.

Something seemed to have been the matter with him, however, because in every town that I rode through I found people just going back to bed after having been aroused up out of their sleep by a mysterious rider. I didn't tell them that it was Mr. Revere, or that it was probably some stunt to do with the shin-dig that he and Mr. Dawes were put-ting on for the North Church. I figured out that it was a little publicity stunt.

Finally, just as I got into Lexington, I saw my man getting off his horse at a house right alongside the Green. I rushed up and caught him just as he was going in. I introduced myself and told him that I represented the Juno Acid Bath Corporation of New York and asked him if he could give me a few minutes, as I had been following him all the way from Charlestown and had been to his office three days in succession. He said that he was busy right at that minute, but that if I wanted to come along with him upstairs he would talk business on the way. He asked me if I wasn't the man he had been talking to at "The Bell in Hand" and I said yes, and asked him how Podunk was. This got him in good humour and he said that we might as well sit right down then and that he would get someone else to do what he had to do. So he called a man-servant and told him to go right upstairs, wake up Mr. Hancock and Mr. Adams and tell them to get up, and no fooling. "Keep after them, Sambo," he said, "and don't let them roll over and go to sleep again. It's very important."

So we sat down in the living room and I got out our statement of sales for 1774 and showed him that, in face of increased competition, Juno had practically doubled its output. "There must be some reason for an acid outselling its competitors three to one," I said, "and that reason, Mr. Revere, is that a Juno product is a guaranteed product." He asked me about the extra sixpence a tin and I asked him if he would rather pay a sixpence less and get an inferior grade of acid and he said, "No." So I finally landed an order of three dozen tins of Vulcan No. 2 and a dozen jars of Acme Silver Polish, as Mr. Revere is a silversmith, also, on the side.

Took a look around Lexington before I went back

to Boston, but didn't see any engraving plants.
Lexington is pretty quiet right now.

Respectfully submitted,

THADDEUS OLIN.

Attached.

Expense Voucher

Juno Acid Bath Corp., New York

Thaddeus Olin, Agent.

Hotel in Boston............................	15s.
Stage fare.................................	30s.
Meals (4 days)............................	28s.
Entertaining prospects....................	£3 4s.
Horse rent. Charlestown to Lexington and return	£2 6s.
	———
Total Expense	£9 3s.
To Profit on three dozen tins of Vulcan No. 2 and	18s.
One dozen jars Acme Silver Polish.........	4s.
	———
	£1 2s.
Net Loss...........................	£8 1s.

FASCINATING CRIMES

I.   *The Odd Occurrence in the Life of Dr. Meethas*

EARLY in the evening of October 14, 1879, Dr.
Attemas Meethas, a physician of good repute
in Elkhart, Indiana, went into the pantry of his
home at 11 Elm Street, ostensibly to see if there was
any of that cold roast pork left.   The good doctor
was given to nibbling cold roast pork when occasion
offered.

As he passed through the living-room on his way
to the pantry, he spoke to his housekeeper, Mrs.
Omphrey, and said that, if everything turned out all
right, he would be at that cold roast pork in about
half a minute (Elkhart time—an hour earlier than
Eastern time).   "Look out for the pits," Mrs. Omphrey cautioned him, and went on with her stitching.
Mrs. Omphrey, in her spare time, was a stitcher of
uppers for the local shoe-factory.

This is the last that was seen of Dr. Attemas
Meethas alive.   It is doubtful if he ever even
reached the pantry, for the cold roast pork was
found untouched on a plate, and Dr. Meethas was
found, three days later, hanging from the top of

the flag-pole on the roof of the Masonic Lodge. The
mystery was even more puzzling in that Dr. Meethas
was not a Mason.

The revolting death of Dr. Meethas.
—*Courtesy of John Held, Jr., and Life.*

Citizens of Elkhart, on being grilled, admitted
having seen the doctor hanging from the flag-pole
for two days, but thought that he was fooling and
would come down soon enough when he got hungry.

But when, after three days, he made no sign of
descending, other than to drop off one shoe, a committee was formed to investigate. It was found that
their fellow-citizen, far from playing a practical
joke on them, had had one played on him, for he was
quite dead, with manifold and singular abrasions. A
particularly revolting feature of the case was that
the little gold chain which the doctor wore over his
right ear, to keep his pince-nez glasses in place, was
still in position. This at once disposed of the possibility of suicide.

Mrs. Omphrey and her uppers were held for examination, as it was understood that she had at one
time made an attempt on the doctor's life, on the
occasion of his pushing her down when they were
skating together. But her story in the present affair
was impregnable. After the doctor had gone through
the living-room on his way to the pantry, she said
that she continued stitching at her machine until
nine o'clock in the evening. She though it a little
odd that Dr. Meethas did not return from the pantry, but figured it out that there was probably quite
a lot of cold roast pork there and that he was
still busy nibbling. At nine o'clock, however, she
stopped work and started on her rounds of the house
to lock up for the night. On reaching the pantry,
she found that her employer was not there, and had

not been there; at least that he had not touched the pork. She thought nothing of it, however, as it occurred to her that the doctor had probably remembered an engagement and had left suddenly by the pantry window in order not to worry her. So, after finishing the cold pork herself, she locked the bread-box and retired for the night. The police, on investigation, found the bread-box locked just as she had said, and so released Mrs. Omphrey.

When the news of Dr. Meethas' accident reached La Porte, Amos W. Meethas, a brother of the victim and a respected citizen of the town, came directly to Elkhart and insisted on an investigation. He said that his brother had accumulated quite a fortune tinting postcards on the side, and was known to have this money hidden in a secret panel in the hammock which hung on the back porch. The police, guided by Mr. Amos Meethas, went to the hammock, slid the panel open and found nothing there but some old clippings telling of Dr. Meethas' confirmation in 1848. (He was a confirmed old bachelor.) This definitely established robbery as the motive for the crime. The next thing to do was to discover someone who could climb flag-poles.

Neighbors of the doctor recalled that some weeks before a young man had gone from door to door asking if anybody wanted his flag-pole climbed. He

Dr. Meethas—The unfortunate victim.
—*Courtesy of John Held, Jr., and Life.*

said he was working his way through college climbing flag-poles and would be grateful for any work, however small. He was remembered to have been a short youth about six feet two or three, with hair blond on one side and dark on the other. This much the neighbors agreed upon.

Working in South Bend at the time was a young man named Herman Trapp. He was apprehended by the authorities, who subsequently decided that he had no connection whatever with the tragedy.

So the strange murder of Dr. Meethas (if indeed it *was* a murder) rests to this day unsolved and forgotten, which is just as well, as it was at best a pretty dull case.

UPSETS

THUS far, the football season of 1927 has been one of upsets. Nothing has turned out according to the dope. Therefore, in its remaining weeks, we predict the following startling deviations from form:

1. It will not rain the day of the Big Game.

2. We shall have no more than a dozen requests for "a couple of seats."

3. Our own seats will be, not in the wooden stands behind the scoreboard, but out in full view of the field. (We have to laugh even when writing this in fun.)

4. There will not be an intoxicated man in a rhinoceros coat directly in front of us who jumps up at the sound of the whistle.

5. There will not be a small man with a 13½ collar behind us who has ideas on how the team should be run.

6. The game will not have started while we are milling around in the crowd at the gate.

7. Nobody will fall down the steps.

8. Holding tickets for two seats, we shall find

that there is space left in which two people can sit without being married to each other.

9. We shall not be too hot above the waist and too cold below.

10. Harvard will win and we shall see ten dollars of Donald Ogden Stewart's money.

AN INTERVIEW WITH MUSSOLINI

MUSSOLINI seemed to be a good man to interview; so I got an interview with him.

"Mr. Mussolini," I said, "as I understand your theory of government, while it is not without its Greek foundations, it dates even farther back, in its essence, to the Assyrian system."

"What?" asked Mussolini.

"I said, as I understood your theory of government, while it is not without its Greek foundations, it dates even farther back to the ancient Assyrian system. Am I right?"

"Assyrian here seen Kelly? K-E-double L-Y. That was a good song, too," said Il Duce.

"A good song is right," I replied. "And now might I ask, how did you come by that beard?"

"That is not a beard," replied the Great Man. "That is my forehead. I am smooth-shaven, as a matter of fact."

"So you are, so you are," I apologized. "I was forgetting."

We both sat silent for a while, thinking of the old days in Syracuse High.

"Whatever became of her?" It was Il Kuce who broke the silence.

"She married and went to Hingham to live," I replied, watching him closely.

He went white for the fraction of a second. Then he turned to me and said:

"Give me your A, will you, please?"

So I gave him my A and we played *"Yes Patineurs"* ("The Skaters"), and very pretty, too.

"I had almost forgotten how it went," he said.

"You *have* forgotten how it went," I corrected him. "You play awful."

Laughter followed this remark of mine. But I noticed that Mussolini was not laughing.

"But about your theory of government," I said, hoping to bring the roses back into those cheeks. "A lot of people try to tell me that it is Phonician, but I always say 'No!'"

"What is it they say it is?" asked Il Huce, all a-tremble with excitement.

"Phœnician," I repeated, putting in the "e."

"That's a tough one," he said. "You'll have to give me a couple of minutes on that. Phœnician, eh? . . . Phœnician drive up in a hack and ask yer." He put this forward tentatively.

"Not so good, Il Duce," I commented.

His eyes filled with tears.

"Oh, well, then," I compromised, "have it your own way."

"I'll have it with plain water, please, and a little lemon-rind." It was the Imperator who spoke.

I signaled to the driver.

"Stop the interview," I said simply.

THE *LIFE* POLAR EXPEDITION

I

IN spite of the fact that already three polar expeditions are well under way in the air, *Life* has decided that the interests of science demand, or at any rate, ask nicely for, an expedition to be conducted through some other medium. We have therefore decided on the bicycle.

We realize that our expedition will have to hurry like everything on bicycles to catch up with the Amundsen and Byrd groups, but we are willing to make the try, and all our men are imbued with an enthusiasm and zeal to carry the banner of *Life* to the Pole which cannot but result in *something*.

Feverish preparations are now under way for the belated start of the *Life* bicycle expedition to the North Pole. The tardy departure has been due to the failure of the contractors to finish the trousers-clips in time, but everything is now in readiness and it looks as if we might start at any minute now. The men are all eager to catch up with Amundsen and Byrd and we all feel that, by very fast pedaling and no fooling along the way, we can do it.

"We *will* do it," Lieutenant Commander Marc Connelly said to me last night, and that just about expresses the spirit behind the whole trip.

"Why did you choose the bicycle?" a lot of people have asked us. "Why *court* danger?"

We realize the risk that we are taking but feel that the bicycle is the logical means for a party of our description to reach the Pole. Three years ago it would have been impossible. But since then we have learned so much more about the earth's magnetism and bicycle navigation that, with the improved technique in balancing which we have developed, we feel that the danger is merely nominal. The farthest that we can possibly fall, in case of an upset, is in an arc with a radius of six feet. Now in this latitude (or in any latitude in which we are likely to be for some time) the rate of acceleration of a falling body is thirty-two feet per second; so you will see that it can't hurt much.

Furthermore, we are using the new Radley model bicycle, which combines all the best features of the old Columbia bicycle with several modern inventions, such as the gyro-balancer and the flash taillight. The gyro-balancer is a contraption attached to the saddle, by means of which the rider is enabled to doze or shell nuts as he rides and be assured that, unless he leans beyond an angle of forty-five degrees, his machine will right itself automatically. If dozing, however, he must not forget to pedal, as the gyro-balancer does not function unless the wheel is in motion. The flash tail-light is more for looks than anything else. It flashes red, green and vanilla.

As at present planned, our course to the Pole will be as follows:

Leave the *Life* office at 598 Madison Ave., New York. Over to Fifth Ave. and up Fifth Ave. to 120th St., skirting Mount Morris Park, past 138th St. (Mott Haven), striking onto the Bronx River Parkway. Up through Morrisania, Woodlawn, Mount Vernon, Bronxville, Tuckahoe, Crestwood, Scarsdale, and Hartsdale to White Plains. From White Plains we continue north direct into Canada and through Canada to Victoria Island. A short carry across Melville Sound to Melville Island. Another carry to Borden Island, followed by a short carry to Axel Heiberg Land and a final carry to Grant Land on Ellesmere Island. Thence direct to the Pole.

2

En route with LIFE's *Polar Expedition, passing through 125th St., Manhattan, May 12.*—After a successful hop-off from the curbing in front of the office of *Life* at 598 Madison Ave., New York City, we pedalled our bicycles slowly up Madison Ave. to 59th St., where it was discovered that Lieut.-Commander Connelly's rear wheel was still locked, a precaution which had been taken while the machines were standing in the rack outside the office. This had made speed out of the question for Lieut.-Commander Connelly, and had resulted in an odd, dragging sensation which he was at a loss to account for until a passer-by called his attention to the locked wheel. The trouble was immediately remedied, and the expedition proceeded at a much smarter pace up Madison Ave.

This little incident, at the very outset of our trip, while unimportant in itself, just goes to show the spirit which is animating our men and the determination in their hearts to see this thing through at any cost. Lieut.-Commander Connelly might very well have become discouraged when he found that his rear wheel was not revolving at all and abandoned the thing entirely, but with characteristic bulldog grit he kept pedalling right ahead with only one wheel and would probably have stuck at it until the Pole was reached, do or die. It is such courage that makes us all optimistic.

Proceeding up Madison Ave. to 60th St., we turned the wheels at a sharp right angle and cut across into Fifth Ave. This, while perhaps fool-

hardy on the face of it, was not the madcap move
that it may seem to you sitting safely at home reading of our progress. For we had received wireless
messages from the station at 72nd St. and Madison
Ave. that at that corner there was a nasty excava-
tion, into which we might very well have hurtled
with disastrous results had we kept on our way up
Madison. "I never before realized what a valuable
service the wireless telegraph can accomplish," said
Ensign Thermaline to me. Ensign Thermaline was
on the bicycle just ahead of me, and as he turned
to make this remark, his front wheel struck the
curbing a glancing blow, which threatened for a
moment to result in a spill, but with rare presence
of mind Ensign Thermaline turned his head front
again without waiting for my corroboration of his
remark (which I would have given willingly had
there been time or had the occasion been more pro-
pitious) and, utilizing the gyro-balancer with which
each of our Radley machines is equipped, righted
himself and his wheel in no time at all. It was an
exciting moment, however, and we all felt better
when Ensign Thermaline was once again headed
straight north up Fifth Ave.

All of our instruments are in excellent working
order except the flash tail-light on Lieut.-Com-
mander Connelly's wheel, which persists in flashing

red, a signal that he is going the other way. It should be flashing green. This has caused a little confusion among vehicles following in our wake, for the printed directions in the daily papers stated that those vehicles encountering our expedition en route could tell the direction in which we were moving by watching our flash tail-lights, red if we were going south and green if we were going north. Something akin to a panic was caused among the passengers on a Fifth Ave. bus which was following close on behind Lieut.-Commander Connelly's wheel when he suddenly flashed red, indicating that he was pedalling head-on for the bus. It was only when Lieut.-Commander Connelly yelled a cheery "Mistake, mistake!" that the bus-driver could be convinced that he ought not to turn aside and let the Connelly wheel pass.

We are now approaching 125th St. and the difference in the atmospheric conditions between lower and upper Fifth Ave. is distinctly noticeable. The traffic, while just as heavy, is a little easier to steer through. Ensign Thermaline seems, at the moment, to be lost, but I have no doubt that he will turn up again as soon as that big van gets out of the way just beyond Capt. Nordney. Capt. Nordney joined the expedition at the Heckscher Foundation at 104th St. and Fifth Ave.

It now looks as if we might be able to make 138th St. (Mott Haven) by night-fall, but I rather hope that we don't as there probably wouldn't be any place to spend the night. I certainly have never seen, or heard of, any hotels in that neighborhood.

* * *

135th St., New York City, May 12.—At 5:58 p. m. today the *Life* Polar Expedition passed through this street, bearing N.E. by N. The members seemed a little tired and Lieut.-Commander Connelly's wheel was dragging badly. Commander Benchley was sending out messages in all directions, asking if anyone knew where they could put up for the night.

* * *

Railroad Y. M. C. A., 140th St., New York City, May 12.—Preparations are being made here to take care of the *Life* Polar Expedition, which is due to make a landing at 6:20 p. m. Searchlights are in readiness and hot baths are being run to accommodate at least two of the party.

THE SAVING-"OLD-IRONSIDES" HABIT

THE annual campaign to "Save 'Old Iron-sides'" is on again. Every few years this ancient frigate is saved from some mysterious destruction, school children are lathered up into a foam of patriotic excitement in which they bring pennies from their banks to aid in the crisis, speeches are made and banners unfurled, and everybody sinks back with a sigh of relief. "Old Ironsides" has been saved again!

And yet it hardly seems more than a couple of years before the cry goes up again: "The enemy!" and bang! a shot whistles across the bows of the famous ship. Then it's "Save 'Old Ironsides,' boys!" and the whole thing begins all over again.

Oliver Wendell Holmes, who aided the first "Save 'Old Ironsides'" campaign by writing, "Ay, tear her tattered ensign down!" must smile a rather wan smile as he realizes that all that he did was save "Old Ironsides" for the fiscal year 1887-8 and that ever since then a Saving Committee has been kept busy night and day planning future campaigns. They say that the 1930 campaign is going to be the biggest and best yet.

What are these malign forces that seem so persist-
ent in their plots to wreck the good ship "Constitution"?   Sometimes it is an unsentimental Government that threatens to junk the whole thing.   At
other times it is the forces of Nature, which seem
to wait until our backs are turned after a money-
raising campaign and then jump at the poor old
sea-dog as she lies in safety at Charlestown and bid
fair to tear her limb from limb.

Whatever it is that we are constantly fighting off,
would it not be possible to raise enough money at
one crack to keep "Old Ironsides" afloat *forever?*
We have a national surplus of $390,000,000.
Couldn't we just settle this whole thing once and for
all by devoting, let us say, half of that to seeing
that no more harm ever comes to this precious relic?

Having saved her three times, and won three legs
on the trophy, might we not be entitled to permanent
possession of it?

Or has the fact that there is a movie entitled
"Old Ironsides" anything to do with what James
Russell Lowell called "The Present Crisis"?

A GOOD OLD-FASHIONED CHRISTMAS

SOONER or later at every Christmas party, just as things are beginning to get good, someone shuts his eyes, puts his head back and moans softly: "Ah, well, this isn't like the old days. We don't seem to have any good old-fashioned Christmases any more." To which the answer from my corner of the room is: "All right! That suits me!"

Just what they have in mind when they say "old-fashioned Christmas" you never can pin them down to telling. "Lots of snow," they mutter, "and lots of food." Yet, if you work it right, you can still get plenty of snow and food today. Snow, at any rate.

Then there seems to be some idea of the old-fashioned Christmas being, of necessity, in the country. It doesn't make any difference whether you were raised on a farm or whether your ideas of a rural Christmas were gleaned from pictures in old copies of "Harper's Young People," you must give folks to understand that such were the surroundings in which you spent your childhood holidays. And that, ah, me, those days will never come again!

Well, supposing you get your wish some time. Supposing, let us say, your wife's folks who live up in East Russet, Vermont, write and ask you to come up and bring the children for a good old-fashioned Christmas, "while we are all still together," they add cheerily with their flair for putting everybody in good humor.

Hurray, hurray! Off to the country for Christmas! Pack up all the warm clothes in the house, for you will need them up there where the air is clean and cold. Snow-shoes? Yes, put them in, or better yet, Daddy will carry them. What fun! Take along some sleigh-bells to jangle in case there aren't enough on the pung. There must be jangling sleigh-bells. And whisky for frost-bite. Or is it snake-bite that whisky is for? Anyway, put it in! We're off! Good-by, all! Good-by! JANGLE - JANGLE - JANGLE - Jangle - Jangle - Jangle-jangle-jangle-jangle-jangle-jangle-jangle!

In order to get to East Russet you take the Vermont Central as far as Twitchell's Falls and change there for Torpid River Junction, where a spur line takes you right into Gormley. At Gormley you are met by a buckboard which takes you back to Torpid River Junction again. By this time a train or something has come in which will wait for the local from Besus. While waiting for this you will have time to

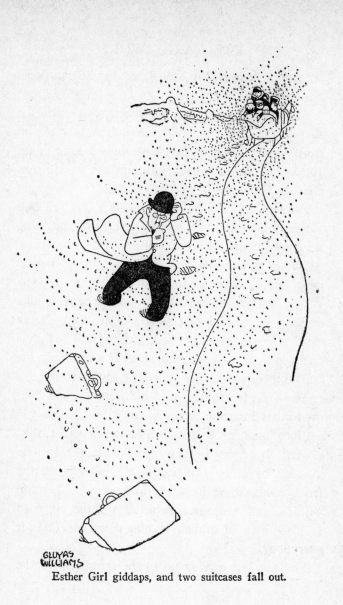

Esther Girl giddaps, and two suitcases fall out.

send your little boy to school, so that he can finish the third grade.

At East Russet Grandpa meets you with the sleigh. The bags are piled in and Mother sits in front with Lester in her lap while Daddy takes Junior and Ga-Ga in back with him and the luggage. Giddap, Esther Girl!

Esther Girl giddaps, and two suitcases fall out. Heigh-ho! Out we get and pick them up, brushing the snow off and filling our cuffs with it as we do so. After all, there is nothing like snow for getting up one's cuffs. Good clean snow never hurt anyone. Which is lucky, because after you have gone a mile or so, you discover that Ga-Ga is missing. Never mind, she is a self-reliant little girl and will doubtless find her way to the farm by herself. Probably she will be there waiting for you when you arrive.

The farm is situated on a hill about eleven hundred miles from the center of town, just before you get into Canada. If there is a breeze in winter, they get it. But what do they care for breezes, so long as they have the Little Colonel oil-heater in the front room, to make everything cozy and warm within a radius of four inches! And the big open fireplace with the draught coming down it! Fun for everybody!

You are just driving up to the farmhouse in the

sleigh, with the entire right leg frozen where the lap robe has slipped out. Grandma is waiting for you at the door and you bustle in, all glowing with good cheer. "Merry Christmas, Grandma!" Lester is cross and Junior is asleep and has to be dragged by the hand upstairs, bumping against each step all the way. It is so late that you decide that you all might as well go to bed, especially as you learn that breakfast is at four-thirty. It usually is at four, but Christmas being a holiday everyone sleeps late.

As you reach the top of the stairs you get into a current of cold air which has something of the quality of the temperature in a nice well-regulated crypt. This is the Bed Room Zone, and in it the thermometer never tops the zero mark from October fifteenth until the middle of May. Those rooms in which no one sleeps are used to store perishable vegetables in, and someone has to keep thumbing the tomatoes and pears every so often to prevent their getting so hard that they crack.

The way to get undressed for bed in one of Grandpa's bedrooms is as follows: Starting from the foot of the stairs where it is warm, run up two at a time to keep the circulation going as long as possible. Opening the bedroom door with one hand, tear down the curtains from the windows with the other, pick up the rugs from the floor and snatch the spread from the top of the bureau. Pile all these on the bed, cover with the closet door which you have wrenched from its hinges, and leap quickly underneath. It sometimes helps to put on a pair of rubbers over your shoes.

And even when you are in bed, you have no guarantee of going to sleep. Grandpa's mattresses seem to contain the overflow from the silo, corn-husks, baked-potato skins and long, stringy affairs which feel like pipe cleaners. On a cold night, snuggling down into these is about like snuggling down into a bed of damp pine cones out in the forest.

Then there are Things abroad in the house. Shortly after you get into bed, the stairs start snap-ping. Next something runs along the roof over your head. You say to yourself: "Don't be silly. It's only Santa Claus." Then it runs along in the wall behind the head of the bed. Santa Claus wouldn't do that. Down the long hall which leads into the ell of the house you can hear the wind sighing softly, with an occasional reassuring bang of a door.

The unmistakable sound of someone dying in great pain rises from just below the window-sill. It is a sort of low moan, with just a touch of strangula-tion in it. Perhaps Santa has fallen off the roof. Perhaps that story you once heard about Grandpa's

house having been a hang-out for Revolutionary
smugglers is true, and one of the smugglers has
come back for his umbrella. The only place at a
time like this is down under the bedclothes. But
the children become frightened and demand to be
taken home, and Grandpa has to be called to explain
that it is only Blue Bell out in the barn. Blue Bell
has asthma, and on a cold night they have to be
very patient with her.

Christmas morning dawns cloudy and cold, with
the threat of plenty more snow, and, after all, what
would Christmas be without snow? You lie in bed
for one hour and a quarter trying to figure out how
you can get up without losing the covers from
around you. A glance at the water pitcher shows
that it is time for them to put the red ball up for
skating. You think of the nice warm bathroom at
home, and decide that you can wait until you get
back there before shaving.

This breaking the ice in the pitcher seems to be a
feature of the early lives of all great men which
they look back on with tremendous satisfaction.
"When I was a boy, I used to have to break the
ice in the pitcher every morning before I could
wash," is said with as much pride as one might say,
"When I was a boy I stood at the head of my class."
Just what virtue there is in having to break ice in a

pitcher is not evident, unless it lies in their taking
the bother to break the ice and wash at all. Any
time that I have to break ice in a pitcher as a pre-

The entire family enters, purple and chattering and
exceedingly cross.

liminary to washing, I go unwashed, that's all. And
Benjamin Franklin and U. S. Grant and Rutherford
B. Hayes can laugh as much as they like. I'm no-
body's fool about a thing like that.

Getting the children dressed is a lot of fun when you have to keep pumping their limbs up and down to keep them from freezing out stiff. The children love it and are just as bright and merry as little pixies when it is time to go downstairs and say "Good morning" to Grandpa and Grandma. The entire family enters the dining-room purple and chattering and exceedingly cross.

After breakfast everyone begins getting dinner. The kitchen being the only warm place in the house may have something to do with it. But before long there are so many potato peelings and turkey feathers and squash seeds and floating bits of pie crust in the kitchen that the women-folk send you and the children off into the front part of the house to amuse yourselves and get out of the way.

Then what a jolly time you and the kiddies and Grandpa have together! You can either slide on the horse-hair sofa, or play "The Wayside Chapel" on the piano (the piano has scroll-work on either side of the music rack with yellow silk showing through), or look out the window and see ten miles of dark gray snow. Perhaps you may even go out to the barn and look at the horses and cows, but really, as you walk down between the stalls, when you have seen one horse or one cow you have seen them all. And besides, the cold in the barn has an added flavor of damp harness leather and musty carriage upholstery which eats into your very marrow.

Of course, there are the presents to be distributed, but that takes on much the same aspect as the same ceremony in the new-fashioned Christmas, except that in the really old-fashioned Christmas the presents weren't so tricky. Children got mostly mittens and shoes, with a sled thrown in sometimes for dissipation. Where a boy today is bored by three o'clock in the afternoon with his electric grain-elevator and miniature pond with real perch in it, the old-fashioned boy was lucky if he got a copy of "Naval Battles of the War of 1812" and an orange. Now this feature is often brought up in praise of the old way of doing things. "I tell you," says Uncle Gyp, "the children in my time never got such presents as you get today." And he seems proud of the fact, as if there were some virtue accruing to him for it. If the children of today can get electric grain-elevators and tin automobiles for Christmas, why aren't they that much better off than their grandfathers who got only wristlets? Learning the value of money, which seems to be the only argument of the stand-patters, doesn't hold very much water as a Christmas slogan. The value of money can be learned in just about five minutes when the time comes, but Christmas is not the season.

But to return to the farm, where you and the kiddies and Gramp' are killing time. You can either bring in wood from the woodshed, or thaw out the pump, or read the books in the bookcase over the writing-desk. Of the three, bringing in the wood will probably be the most fun, as you are likely to burn yourself thawing out the pump, and the list of reading matter on hand includes "The Life and Deeds of General Grant," "Our First Century," "Andy's Trip to Portland," bound volumes of the Jersey Cattle Breeders' Gazette and "Diseases of the Horse." Then there are some old copies of "Round the Lamp" for the years 1850-54 and some colored plates showing plans for the approaching World's Fair at Chicago.

Thus the time passes, in one round of gayety after another, until you are summoned to dinner. Here all caviling must cease. The dinner lives up to the advertising. If an old-fashioned Christmas could consist entirely of dinner without the old-fashioned bedrooms, the old-fashioned pitcher, and the old-fashioned entertainments, we professional pessimists wouldn't have a turkey-leg left to stand on. But, as has been pointed out, it is possible to get a good dinner without going up to East Russet, Vt., or, if it isn't, then our civilization has been a failure.

And the dinner only makes the aftermath seem

worse.   According to an old custom of the **human**
race, everyone overeats.   Deliberately and **with** con-

Then you sit and moan.

siderable gusto you sit at the table and say pleasantly: "My, but I won't be able to walk after this.
Just a little more of the dark meat, please, Grandpa,
and just a dab of stuffing.   Oh, dear, that's too

much!" You haven't the excuse of the drunkard, who becomes oblivious to his excesses after several drinks. You know what you are doing, and yet you make light of it and even laugh about it as long as you *can* laugh without splitting out a seam.

And then you sit and moan. If you were having a good new-fashioned Christmas you could go out to the movies or take a walk, or a ride, but to be really old-fashioned you must stick close to the house, for in the old days there were no movies and no automobiles and if you wanted to take a walk you had to have the hired man go ahead of you with a snow-shovel and make a tunnel. There are probably plenty of things to do in the country today, and just as many automobiles and electric lights as there are in the city, but you can't call Christmas with all these improvements "an old-fashioned Christmas." That's cheating.

If you are going through with the thing right, you have got to retire to the sitting-room after dinner and *sit*. Of course, you can go out and play in the snow if you want to, but you know as well as I do that this playing in the snow is all right when you are small but a bit trying on anyone over thirty. And anyway, it always began to snow along about three in the afternoon an old-fashioned Christmas day, with a cheery old leaden sky overhead and a jolly old gale sweeping around the corners of the house.

No, you simply must sit indoors, in front of a fire if you insist, but nevertheless with nothing much to do. The children are sleepy and snarling. Grandpa is just sleepy. Someone tries to start the conversation, but everyone else is too gorged with food to be able to move the lower jaw sufficiently to articulate. It develops that the family is in possession of the loudest-ticking clock in the world and along about four o'clock it begins to break its own record. A stenographic report of the proceedings would read as follows:

"Ho-hum!   I'm sleepy!   I shouldn't have eaten so much."

"Tick-tock-tick-tock-tick-tock-tick-tock—"

"It seems just like Sunday, doesn't it?"

"Look at Grandpa!   He's asleep."

"Here, Junior!   Don't plague Grandpa.   Let him sleep."

"Tick-tock-tick-tock-tick-tock—"

"Junior!   Let Grandpa alone!   Do you want Mamma to take you up-stairs?"

"Ho-hum!"

"Tick-tock-tick-tock-tick-tock—"

Louder and louder the clock ticks, until something snaps in your brain and you give a sudden leap into the air with a scream, finally descending to strangle each of the family in turn, and Grandpa as he sleeps. Then, as you feel your end is near, all the warm things you have ever known come back to you, in a flash. You remember the hot Sunday subway to Coney, your trip to Mexico, the bull-fighters of Spain.

You dash out into the snowdrifts and plunge along until you sink exhausted. Only the fact that this article ends here keeps you from freezing to death, with an obituary the next day reading:

"DIED suddenly, at East Russet, Vt., of an old-fashioned Christmas."

LIFE IN THE RITZ TENEMENT

[A recent ruling of the Tenement House Commission places all of New York's new apartment-houses in the technical classification of "tenements" for the enforcement of certain clauses of the Tenement House Law.]

SCENE: *The rear of Mr. Brisbane's new apartment palace—the Ritz Tower. It is Monday morning and the tenants are seen hanging out their wash from the kitchen windows.*

TWENTY-FIRST FLOOR BACK: Good morning to you, Mrs. Van Cleve! A charming day, isn't it?

TWENTY-SECOND FLOOR BACK: The same to you, Mrs. Thornton-Martin. And too charming a day to be cooped up inside like this.

TWENTY-FIRST FLOOR: My *dear,* the killingest thing! Speaking of being cooped up—did you hear that (*lowering the voice*) Freddie Welt was arrested Saturday?

TWENTY-SECOND FLOOR: The Welts on the thirty-fifth floor! My *dear,* how frightful! What for?

TWENTY-FIRST: Well, it seems that Freddie and some of the boys from the Linx Club had been playing polo—

56

"Good morning to you, Mrs. Van Cleve!"

(*A delivery boy from Cartier's clatters up the back stairway.*)

BOY: Van Buren live here?

THIRTIETH FLOOR: Two flights up. They're out now. You can leave the stuff here.

BOY: Three thousand dollars collect on it.

THIRTIETH FLOOR: Go on up and tuck it under the door.

TWENTY-NINTH FLOOR: I'm going to speak to the janitor about those folks on the twenty-eighth.

THIRTIETH FLOOR: A lot of good it will do. They're his cousins. What have they done now?

TWENTY-NINTH FLOOR: All their empty champagne bottles out by the back door where Reggie stumbles over them going to work in the morning! They had a lot of Roumanians up there last night till four in the morning.

THIRTIETH FLOOR: Roumanians, eh? Why don't those people go back where they came from if they don't like it here?

TWENTY-NINTH FLOOR: That's what I'd like to know. I said to Reggie last night, I said, "Reggie, if you were half a man you'd go down there and tell them that if they can't behave themselves why don't they go over to the Racquet Club where they belong."

TWENTY-EIGHTH FLOOR (*flinging open her window*): Oh, is that so?

TWENTY-NINTH FLOOR: Yes, that's so!

TWENTY-EIGHTH FLOOR: Well, if you'd keep that person with the fiddle quiet once in a while the rest of us might get some rest.

TWENTY-NINTH FLOOR (*to the shaft in general*): She calls Jascha Heifetz "that person with a fiddle!"

TWENTY-EIGHTH FLOOR: Jascha Heifetz or Mischa Elman—it's all the same to me. Don't he get enough money playing in concerts that he should come around playing at people's tenements all the time?

THIRTY-FOURTH FLOOR (*slamming open the window*): Shut up below there, will you! (*Throws out a pan full of alligator pear rinds.*)

THE POLICEMAN ON THE BEAT (*from below*): Come on up there, cut that out or I'll run yez all in!

(*All the heads are drawn in and the windows slammed shut.*)

A VOICE ON THE STAIRS WITH BELL ACCOMPANIMENT: Oyster-forks sharpened! Oyster-forks sharpened!

OLD PROGRAM FROM THE BENCHLEY COLLECTION

*A Glance Backward in the Manner of the Authors of
Theatrical Reminiscences*

FEW, probably, of my readers, will remember the
time when the old Forrest Theater stood where
the Central Park Reservoir now is. In those days,
Central Park was considered 'way downtown, or
"crosstown," as they called it then, and one of the
larks of the period was going "down to Central Park
to see the turtles." There was a large turtle farm
in the Park at that time, run by Anderson M. Ferderber, and it was this turtle farm, expanding and
growing as the turtles became more venturesome,
which later became the Zoological Exhibit.

I remember very well the night when it was announced at the Forrest Theater that the building
was to be torn down to make way for the new
Reservoir. It was, as I recall, H. M. Ramus
("Henry" Ramus) who made the announcement.
He was playing *Laertes* at the time (*Laertes* was
played with the deuces wild and a ten-cent limit)
when the manager of the theater (Arthur Semden,

who later became Harrison Blashforth) came into the dressing-room and said: "Well, boys, it's all over. They're going to build the Reservoir here!" There was a silence for a full minute—probably more, for the manager had come into the wrong dressing-room and there was nobody there.

At any rate, "Henry" Ramus was selected to go out and tell the audience. He did it with infinite tact, explaining that there was no need for alarm or panic, as the water could not possibly be let in until the theater was down and the Reservoir constructed, but the audience was evidently taking no chances on being drowned, for within three minutes from the time Ramus began speaking everyone in the theater was outdoors and in a hansom cab. Audience psychology is a queer thing, and possibly this audience knew best. At any rate, the old Forrest Theater is no more.

Speaking of "Henry" Ramus, an amusing anecdote is told of Whitney Hersh. Hersh was playing with Booth in Philadelphia at the time, and was well known for his ability to catch cold, a characteristic which won him many new friends but lost him several old ones. The theater where Booth was playing in *The Queen's Quandary, or What's Open Can't Be Shut*, was the old Chestnut Street Opera House which stood at the corner of what was then Arch,

UP AND AWAY

OR NOBODY KNOWS BUT NERO

OR THREE TIMES SIX IS EIGHTEEN

(Choice of any two titles)

Jonathan Henchman, father of Ralph Henchman and Mother of Men, Old Yale.......	MR. MACREADY
Ralph Henchman, father of Jonathan Henchman and a rather wild young chap....	MR. JUNIUS BOOTH
Jack Wyman, M.D., a doctor who has more "patience" than "patients".............	MR. EDMUND KEENE
Professor Hawksworth, an irascible old fellow who specializes in bird troubles.....	MR. HORNBLOW
Professor Hawksworth, an irascible old fellow who specializes in bird troubles.....	MR. JUNIUS BOOTH
Meeker, a party who lives by his wits and not much of that	MR. JONATHAN EDWARDS
Eugenia, daughter of Jonathan Henchman...........	MRS. SIDDONS
Mlle. de Bon-Ton, a young lady who is not above drinking a little champagne now and then..................	MISS CUSHMAN
Eliza, maid at the Nortons...	BY HERSELF
Hamlet, Prince of Denmark..	MR. WILLIAM A. BRADY

Chestnut, Spruce, Pine and Curly Maple Streets.
This theater was noted in the profession for its
slanting stage, so much so, in fact, that Booth, on
hearing that they were to play there, is said to have
remarked: "The Chestnut Street, eh?" On being
assured that he had heard correctly, Booth simply
smiled. He later founded the Player's Club.

In *The Queen's Quandary, or What's Open Can't
Be Shut,* Hersh had to play the part of *Rodney
Ransome,* the father of several people. In the second act there was a scene in which *Rodney* had to
say to *Marian:*

"But I thought you said the Duke *had* no mous-
tache!"

To which *Marian* was supposed to reply: "I
never was more serious in all my life."

On the night of the opening performance Hersh
was, as usual, very nervous. He got through the
first act all right, with the aid of several promptings
from his mother who was sitting in the balcony.
But when the second act came along, it was evident
to the other members of the company that Hersh
could not be relied upon. This feeling was strength-
ened by the fact that he was nowhere to be found.
They searched high and low for him but, like the
sword of Damocles, he had disappeared. At the
curtain to the second act, however, he was discov-

ered sitting out front in D-113 applauding loudly and calling out: "Hersh! We-want-Hersh!" The only way they could get him back on the stage was a ruse which was not without its pathetic side. The manager of the house stepped out in front of the curtain and asked if any member of the audience would volunteer to come upon the stage and be hypnotized. Hersh, who had always wanted to go on the stage, was one of the first to push his way up. Once behind the footlights again his nervousness left him and he went on with his part where he had left off. It did not fit in with the rest of the play, but they were all so glad to have him back in the cast again that they said nothing about it to him, and whenever, in later years, he himself mentioned the affair, it was always as "that time in Philadelphia when I was so nervous." . . . And that little girl was Charlotte Cushman.

It was at this time that Stopford's *A New Way With Old Husbands, or The Mysterious Drummer-Boy,* was given its first performance at the old Garrick Theater in New York. The old Garrick Theater was torn down in 1878 to make way for the new Garrick Theater, which, in its turn, was torn down in 1880 to make way for the old Garrick again. It is the old, or new, Garrick which now stands at Broadway and Tenth Street on the spot

known to passers-by as "Wanamaker's." Thus is
the silver cord loosed and the pitcher broken at the
well.

*A New Way With Old Husbands, or The Myste-
rious Drummer-Boy* was written for Ada Rehan, but
she was in Fall River at the time; so the part was
given to a young woman who had come to the theater that morning asking if a Mr. Wasserman lived
there. On being told that it was not a private
dwelling and that there was no one there named
Wasserman, she had said:

"Well, then, does anyone here want to subscribe
to the *Saturday Evening Post?*"

Those members of the cast who had gathered on
the bare stage for rehearsal were so impressed by
the young woman's courage that a purse was taken
up for her children in case she had any and, in case
she had no children, for her next of kin.

"I do not want money," she said, taking it. "All
I want is a chance to prove my ability on the stage."

"Can you make the sound of crashing glass?"
asked Arthur Reese, the stage manager.

"I think so," replied the young woman without
looking up.

Reese looked at Meany, the assistant stage manager. "She is the one we want," he said quietly.

So the young woman was engaged. . . . Some

thirty years later the Empire Theater in New York was aglow with lights on the occasion of the opening of *Call the Doctor*. Gay ladies, bejeweled and bejabbered, were running back and forth in the lobby, holding court, while tall, dark gentlemen in evening dress danced attendance. Those who couldn't dance sat it out. It was the metropolitan season at its height.

Suddenly a man burst excitedly through the crowd and made his way to the box-office.

"This seat is ridiculous," he exclaimed to the Treasurer of the theater (Roger M. Wakle, at the time). "I can't even see the stage from it."

"That is not so strange as it may seem to you at first," replied Wakle, "for the curtain is not up yet."

A hush fell over the crowded lobby. This was followed somewhat later by a buzz of excitement. This, in turn, was followed by a detail of mounted police. Men looked at women and at each other. . . . For that young man was Charlotte Cushman.

It was about this time, as I remember it (or maybe later) that the old Augustin Daly Stock Company was at the top of its popularity and everyone was excited over the forthcoming production of *Up and Away*. It had been in rehearsal for several weeks when Tom Nevers asked Daly how much longer they were going to rehearse.

"Oh, about another week," replied Daly, with that old hat which later made him famous.

You can imagine Nevers' feelings!

A glance at the cast assembled for this production might be of interest in the light of subsequent events (the completion of the vehicular tunnel and the Centennial Exposition). So anyway it is in the middle of page 57 to look at if you want to.

As it turned out, *Up and Away* was never produced, as it was found to be too much trouble. But the old Augustin Daly Stock Company will not soon be forgotten.

My memories of St. Louis are of the pleasantest. We played there in Dante's *Really Mrs. Warrington* —and *Twelfth Night*. The *St. Louis Post-Dispatch*, on the morning following our opening, said:

"It is quite probable that before the end of the year we shall see the beginning of the end of the work on the McNaffen Dam. The project has been under construction now for three years and while there can be no suspicion thrown on the awarding of the contracts, nevertheless we must say that the work has progressed but slowly."

It was while we were playing in St. Louis that the news came of the capture of J. Wilkes Booth. A performance of *Richelieu* was in progress, in which I was playing *Rafferty,* and Fanny Davenport the *Queen*. In the second act there is a scene in which *Rafferty* says to *La Pouce:*

> *"I can not, tho' my tongue were free,*
> *Repeat the message that my liege inspires,*
> *And tho' you ask it, were it mine,*
> *And hope you'll be my Valentine."*

Following this speech, *Rafferty* falls down and opens up a bad gash in his forehead.

We had come to this scene on the night I mention, when I noticed that the audience was tittering. I could not imagine what the matter was, and naturally thought of all kinds of things—sheep jumping over a fence—anything. But strange as it may seem, the tittering continued, and I have never found out, from that day to this what amused them so. . . . This was in 1878.

And now we come to the final curtain. For, after all, I sometimes think that Life is like a stage itself. The curtain rises on our little scene; we have our exits and our entrances, and each man in his time plays many parts. I must work this simile up sometime.

Life and the Theater. Who knows? *Selah.*

WHAT COLLEGE DID TO ME

An Outline of Education

MY college education was no haphazard affair. My courses were all selected with a very definite aim in view, with a serious purpose in mind —no classes before eleven in the morning or after two-thirty in the afternoon, and nothing on Saturday at all. That was my slogan. On that rock was my education built.

As what is known as the Classical Course involved practically no afternoon laboratory work, whereas in the Scientific Course a man's time was never his own until four p. m. anyway, I went in for the classic. But only such classics as allowed for a good sleep in the morning. A man has his health to think of. There is such a thing as being a studying fool.

In my days (I was a classmate of the founder of the college) a student could elect to take any courses in the catalogue, provided no two of his choices came at the same hour. The only things he was not supposed to mix were Scotch and gin. This was known as the Elective System. Now I understand that the boys have to have, during the four years, at least three courses beginning with the same letter. This probably makes it very awkward for those who like to get away of a Friday afternoon for the week-end.

Under the Elective System my schedule was somewhat as follows:

Mondays, Wednesdays and Fridays at 11:00:
    Botany 2a (The History of Flowers and Their Meaning)
Tuesdays and Thursdays at 11:00:
    English 26 (The Social Life of the Minor Sixteenth Century Poets)
Mondays, Wednesdays and Fridays at 12:00:
    Music 9 (History and Appreciation of the Clavichord)
Tuesdays and Thursdays at 12:00:
    German 12b (Early Minnesingers—Walter von Vogelweider, Ulric Glannsdorf and Freimann von Stremhofen. Their Songs and Times)
Mondays, Wednesdays and Fridays at 1:30:
    Fine Arts 6 (Doric Columns: Their Uses, History and Various Heights)
Tuesdays and Thursdays at 1:30:
    French 1c (Exceptions to the verb *être*)

This was, of course, just one year's work. The next year I followed these courses up with supplementary courses in the history of lace-making, Russian taxation systems before Catharine the Great,

North American glacial deposits and Early Renaissance etchers.

Some of the drawings in my economics notebook were the finest things I have ever done.

This gave me a general idea of the progress of civilization and a certain practical knowledge which has stood me in good stead in thousands of ways since my graduation.

My system of studying was no less strict. In lecture courses I had my notebooks so arranged that one-half of the page could be devoted to drawings of five-pointed stars (exquisitely shaded), girls' heads, and tick-tack-toe. Some of the drawings in my economics notebook in the course on Early English Trade Winds were the finest things I have ever done. One of them was a whole tree (an oak) with every leaf in perfect detail. Several instructors commented on my work in this field.

These notes I would take home after the lecture, together with whatever supplementary reading the course called for. Notes and textbooks would then be placed on a table under a strong lamplight. Next came the sharpening of pencils, which would take perhaps fifteen minutes. I had some of the best sharpened pencils in college. These I placed on the table beside the notes and books.

At this point it was necessary to light a pipe, which involved going to the table where the tobacco was. As it so happened, on the same table was a poker hand, all dealt, lying in front of a vacant chair. Four other chairs were oddly enough occupied by students, also preparing to study. It therefore resolved itself into something of a seminar, or group conference, on the courses under discussion. For example, the first student would say:

"I can't open."

The second student would perhaps say the same thing.

The third student would say: "I'll open for fifty cents."

And the seminar would be on.

At the end of the seminar, I would go back to my desk, pile the notes and books on top of each other, put the light out, and go to bed, tired but happy in the realization that I had not only spent the evening busily but had helped put four of my friends through college.

An inventory of stock acquired at college discloses the following bits of culture and erudition which have nestled in my mind after all these years.

THINGS I LEARNED FRESHMAN YEAR

1. Charlemagne either died or was born or did something with the Holy Roman Empire in 800.

2. By placing one paper bag inside another paper bag you can carry home a milk shake in it.

3. There is a double l in the middle of "parallel."

4. Powder rubbed on the chin will take the place of a shave if the room isn't very light.

5. French nouns ending in "aison" are feminine.

6. Almost everything you need to know about a subject is in the encyclopedia.

7. A tasty sandwich can be made by spreading peanut butter on raisin bread.

8. A floating body displaces its own weight in the liquid in which it floats.

9. A sock with a hole in the toe can be worn inside out with comparative comfort.

10. The chances are against filling an inside straight.

11. There is a law in economics called *The Law of Diminishing Returns,* which means that after a certain margin is reached returns begin to diminish. This may not be correctly stated, but there *is* a law by that name.

12. You begin tuning a mandolin with A and tune the other strings from that.

SOPHOMORE YEAR

1. A good imitation of measles rash can be effected by stabbing the forearm with a stiff whiskbroom.

2. Queen Elizabeth was not above suspicion.

3. In Spanish you pronounce z like th.

4. Nine-tenths of the girls in a girls' college are not pretty.

5. You can sleep undetected in a lecture course by resting the head on the hand as if shading the eyes.

6. Weakness in drawing technique can be hidden by using a wash instead of black and white line.

7. Quite a respectable bun can be acquired by smoking three or four pipefuls of strong tobacco when you have no food in your stomach.

8. The ancient Phœnicians were really Jews, and got as far north as England where they operated tin mines.

9. You can get dressed much quicker in the morning if the night before when you are going to bed you take off your trousers and underdrawers at once, leaving the latter inside the former.

JUNIOR YEAR

1. Emerson left his pastorate because he had some argument about communion.

2. All women are untrustworthy.

3. Pushing your arms back as far as they will go fifty times each day increases your chest measurement.

4. Marcus Aurelius had a son who turned out to be a bad boy.

5. Eight hours of sleep are not necessary.

6. Heraclitus believed that fire was the basis of all life.

7. A good way to keep your trousers pressed is to hang them from the bureau drawer.

8. The chances are that you will never fill an inside straight.

9. The Republicans believe in a centralized government, the Democrats in a de-centralized one.

10. It is not necessarily effeminate to drink tea.

SENIOR YEAR

1. A dinner coat looks better than full dress.

2. There is as yet no law determining what constitutes trespass in an airplane.

3. Six hours of sleep are not necessary.

4. Bicarbonate of soda taken before retiring makes you feel better the next day.

5. You needn't be fully dressed if you wear a cap and gown to a nine-o'clock recitation.

6. Theater tickets may be charged.

7. Flowers may be charged.

8. May is the shortest month in the year.

The foregoing outline of my education is true enough in its way, and is what people like to think about a college course. It has become quite the cynical thing to admit laughingly that college did one no good. It is part of the American Credo that all that the college student learns is to catch punts and dance. I had to write something like that to satisfy the editors. As a matter of fact, I learned a great deal in college and have those four years to thank for whatever I know today.

(The above note was written to satisfy those of my instructors and financial backers who may read this. As a matter of fact, the original outline is true, and I had to look up the date about Charlemagne at that.)

AN INTERVIEW WITH THEODORE DREISER

I FOUND the author of "An American Tragedy" reading a large volume of law reports.

"Working on a new book?" I asked.

"It's a new book to me," replied Dreiser. "I don't know about you."

"Oh, I'm all right," I retorted. "A little dizzy when I stand up—but then, one doesn't have to stand up much, does one?"

"Does two, does three, does four," sallied the author, up to one hundred.

I could see that we were treading on dangerous ground and, fearful lest the interview be ruined, I continued, wetting my thumb:

"Do you get around to the night clubs much?"

"Much more than what?" asked Mr. Dreiser.

"I didn't say 'much more than' anything. I just said 'much.' "

"Well, you took a very funny way of saying it," said the pioneer. And added, "I *must* say."

Things had reached an *impasse*. The storm which had been gathering for centuries between Church and State was about to break, and with it the temporal power of Rome.

"Let's get out of here!" I said, taking Dreiser by the arm. "I don't like the looks of things."

"Someone was saying that very thing to me only yesterday," said the author of "The Genius." "Now who was it?"

"George Erlich?" I suggested.

"No," said Dreiser.

"Roger Hatney?"

"No."

"Mrs. Federber?"

"No, no! For God's sake, man, try and *think!*"

"Wentworth Whamer?"

"No."

"Ernst Timmerley?"

"That's who it was! Ernst Timmerley! How stupid of me not to remember. Ernst Timmerley, that's who it was."

"I thought of suggesting him at first," I said, "but it slipped my mind."

"You can't tell me that was just a coincidence," said the author of "Sister Carrie."

"Oh, I can't, can't I?" I retorted, not a little piqued. "Well, *it was just a coincidence.*"

Dreiser looked at me half quizzically.

"You win," he said simply.

Outside the snow was blowing down the street like an army of fireflies, but inside, by the fire, it was warm.

FASCINATING CRIMES

II. The Wallack Disappearances

SHORTLY after the Civil War the residents of Wallack, Connecticut, were awakened by the barking of a dog belonging to James Lenn, a visiting farmer. The dog was an old one, so they thought nothing of it, and went back to sleep again.

Later it was discovered that James Lenn was missing, and that the dog also had disappeared, but in the opposite direction. A search of the countryside was instituted which resulted in the finding of twenty-five empty tins, several old brooms, enough newspapers to make a fair-sized bale, and one old buggy-top. None of these seemed to have any value as clews in the mysterious disappearance of James Lenn. Some importance was attached to the discovery of the buggy-top until it was found that the missing farmer was not hiding under it.

The police, however, were not satisfied. There had been several violations of the State Fishing and Gaming ordinances in and around Wallack and public censure of the police was at its height. Chief of Police Walter M. Turbot determined to carry this

case through to a finish. Thus it was that the search
for Farmer James Lenn was begun afresh, a search
which was destined to end in Innsbruck, Austria.

In the little town of Innsbruck there had been
living an old garbler named Leon Nabgratz, a sort
of town character, if such a thing were possible.

The principles in the famous Wallack disappearances.
—*Courtesy of John Held, Jr., and Life.*

Nabgratz had never been to America, but his young
nephew, Gurling Nabgratz, son of Leon's brother
Meff, was born in that country and had lived there
all his life. Late in December, 1867, he had moved
to Wallack, Connecticut, where he was sold as a
slave to one James Lenn.

One day, while reading the newspaper, Gurling
Nabgratz came across an item indicating that slavery
had been abolished four years previously and figured
out that he was just a sap to be working for James

Lenn for nothing. He mentioned the matter to his master, but Lenn maintained that it was only the Negro slaves who had been freed, and that Lincoln was no longer President anyway.

Nabgratz went away grumbling but did his chores that day as usual. He was seen late in the evening of April 17 in the poolroom of the village, where he is said to have made *sotto-voce* remarks and sung several slave songs of the ante-bellum South with such inflammatory refrains as "We'se all gwine ter be free!"

That night Gurling Nabgratz disappeared and was never seen again in Wallack.

This having preceded the disappearance of James Lenn by about two years, nothing was thought of it at the time. During the search for Lenn, however, the incident was recalled, and a search for Nabgratz was instituted. This made two searches going on at once in the little town of Wallack, and resulted in considerable hard feeling between the rival search-ing-parties. The town was divided into two camps, the "Find Lenn" faction and the "Find Nabgratz" faction, and on at least one occasion shots were exchanged.

In the meantime, in Innsbruck, Austria, Leon Nabgratz, the old garbler, was quietly pursuing his way, quite unconscious of the stir that he was caus-

ing four thousand miles away. His brother Meff
had written him about Gurling's disappearance, but,
as the old man never bothered to read his brother's
letters, he was just as much in the dark as he had
been before. More so, in fact, because he was older.

His surprise can well be imagined, therefore, when
one day in the spring of 1869 the police entered his
house in the Schmalzgasse and began a search for
James Lenn of Wallack, Connecticut, U. S. A. In
vain Nabgratz protested that he had never heard the
name of Lenn and that, even if he had, it was not
interesting to him. The arm of the law reaching
across the Atlantic was inexorable. Leon Nabgratz's house was searched and in it was found an
old trunk of suspiciously large proportions. In spite
of the fact that this trunk was labeled *"Weihnachts-
geschenke"* ("Christmas presents") it was opened,
and in it were found James Lenn *and* Gurling Nabgratz, together with a copy of the New York *Times*
of October 12, 1868.

The mysterious Wallack disappearances were thus
explained, and Leon Nabgratz was arrested for having in his possession a trunk with a misleading label
on it.

Art is long and time is fleeting.

LOUIS DOT DOPE

ON his recent return from France, Mr. Robert Benchley gave the following statement to reporters who met him at Quarantine with bail.

"Things in France are in a deplorable condition," said Mr. Benchley. "If Louis XVI keeps on as he has been going for the past few years, I predict a revolution. I can give you no idea of the licentiousness and waste of the French Court at Versailles or of the pitiable state of the common people in Paris. Yes, I can too give you *some* idea, and, what is more, I *will*.

"This Louis XVI is nothing but a wastrel. He drinks a great deal, too. And he has gathered about him at Versailles (where he lives) a group of sycophants who are just as bad as he is, according to all reports. I am not one to retail gossip, but I could tell you some of the things that go on out there at Versailles that would make your hair stand on end. And, in the meantime, the people in Paris are actually starving. You can't get an oyster stew in Paris for love or money, and I have seen the *canaille* (as the log-rolling wits of the Court call the citizenry) standing in line for hours for something, I couldn't quite make out what.

"One little incident that I heard of from a pretty good source (Carlyle: page 375) may serve to illustrate the way the wind is blowing. It seems that Louis (as his toadies call him) was out driving through Paris with his—pardon me—mistress (I mention no names) when the people began crying out for bread. The 'lady' in question, who can read French and speak it but who has difficulty in understanding it when it is spoken fast, asked what it was that they were yelling. Louis told her that they said they had no more bread. 'Let them eat cake then,' said this certain party. 'And how about us taking a look in at Cartier's window?'

"I don't know how true this is, but I got it from someone on the inside and it shows pretty well the attitude of the nobles towards the common people.

"But there is an undercurrent of discontent which I predict will make itself felt before many months. I happened to go to lunch with a couple of chaps whose names, for obvious reasons, I promised not to mention in this connection, and there was a great deal of talk about how easy it would be to burn down the Bastille (the government jail over there). 'A couple of good pushes and the Bastille would fall,' said one of them jokingly. But behind all their joking there was a note of seriousness, and I would recommend that you send a good man over to Paris pretty soon to cover the story, for when it breaks it is going to be a hot one. This is just a tip.

"But, as I was saying, it is out there at Versailles that the big doings go on. I took a trip out there with a letter from Whitney Warren, but they were all out at Chantilly at the races that day and I didn't see anyone but the Head Guide. He said that if I wanted to come back Sunday the fountains would be playing, but unfortunately I had to sail on Saturday. I did get some inside dope on the situation out there, however, and let me tell you that what goes on out there on a good night is nobody's business. All these people, it seems, live right out there in the palace together and carry on some pretty rough stuff, I gather. Drinking, gambling, necking, *everything*. A lot of the married men are out there without their wives, and *vice versa*. Some nights the parties don't break up until two and three o'clock. No wonder the taxpayers in Paris are sore. You can mark my words, there will be a reaction.

"I myself didn't have time to get around much. I was over on business and I like to keep my head clear when I have business to attend to. Summer is when I have my fun. I did go to the theater a couple of times, but everything was in French. And then, too, the coffee is so bad there. The trip back was pretty rough. One day the waves were mountain-high. It certainly seems good to be back in the U. S. A. again."

THE RISE AND FALL OF THE
CHRISTMAS CARD

TWENTY-FIVE years ago (December 21, 1685, to be exact) a man named Ferderber awoke after a week's business trip and realized that he hadn't bought any Christmas presents for his relatives and friends. Furthermore, all he had left from the business trip was eighty cents, two theater-ticket stubs, and a right shoe.

So he cut up some cardboard to fit envelopes and on each card wrote some little thought for the season. Being still a trifle groggy, he thought that it would be nice to make them rhyme although, as he expressed it, with a modest smile, "I am no poet."

The one to his aunt read as follows:

"Just a little thought of cheer,
A Merry Christmas and a Happy New Year."

He liked this one so well that he just copied it on all the others. Then he got excited about the thing and drew a sprig of holly on each card. He mailed them on Christmas Eve and discovered that he still had twenty-eight cents left.

This man Ferderber is now wanted in thirty-two

states on the same charge: Starting the Christmas
Card Menace. His idea immediately took hold of

He liked this one so well he just copied it on all the others.

the public imagination and the next Christmas all
his friends and relatives sent cards to their friends

and relatives, for, taking the old lie that "it isn't so much the gift as the spirit i.w.i.i.g." at its face value, they felt that people would be much better pleased with a friendly greeting than with a nasty old gift. And, for a while, the custom really was quite a relief.

Then the thing began to get out of hand. Big Christmas card manufacturing concerns sprang up all over the country and factory sites adjacent to freight sidings were at a premium. Millions and millions of cards were printed and millions and millions of people began sending them to each other. Along about December 15, the blight began and, like locusts, the envelopes started drifting in from the mail. Seventy-five thousand extra mail carriers were drafted into service and finally the Government was forced to commandeer all males under 25 who did not have flat feet. Even at that, all the Christmas cards couldn't be delivered until the first of the year, and by that time the flood of New Year's cards had begun, for everyone who received Christmas cards from people to whom they had sent none rushed out and bought New Year's cards to send them the next week just as if that was what they had intended to do all along.

It became impossible to read all these cards, and finally even to open them. Great stacks of unopened envelopes covered desks and hall tables throughout the country. Some of the wealthier citizens had chutes built on the outside of their houses into which the post men dumped the cards and by means of which they were conveyed direct to the furnace. The poorer people, unable to convert their mail matter into fuel in this manner, unable sometimes to clear away a path from their front door to the street, often starved to death before their provisions could be got to them. The winter of 1927 was known as the Winter of the Red Death, for all over the country families were snowed in with envelopes and perished before help could be brought to them. In some towns fires were accidentally started with results too horrible to relate.

UNEARTH VALUABLE SCIENTIFIC DATA

Excavators who have recently been at work in the Middle West digging through mounds of petrified envelopes have furnished valuable data on the nature of these *objets d'art*. The most popular design seems to have been that involving a fireplace with stockings hanging from it, with the slogan, evidently satirical, "A Merry Christmas and a Happy New Year." Candles were also highly considered as decoration; candles and bells. When human figures were introduced, they were of the most unpleasant types: short, fat, bearded men dressed in red, offensively gay little children in pajamas carrying lighted candles, stagecoaches filled with steaming travelers, sleigh rides and coasting parties, and street musicians annoying householders with Christmas carols. The text was usually in Old English type, so that fortunately it was difficult, if not impossible, to read.

Evidently the tide began to turn when some one, perhaps a descendant of the very Ferderber who had brought all this distress on the land, thought of the idea of venting his personal spleen in his Christmas cards. He thought that, since no one read them anyway, he might as well say what he really felt, so long as he said it in Old English type. It would be a satisfaction to him, anyway. So near the top of these mounds of Early Twentieth Century cards we find some on this order:

A picture of a holly wreath with a large hammer stuck through it and the following legend:

"Just to Wish You the Measles.
Christmas 1931."

Another showed a little cottage on the brow of a snow-covered hill with the sun setting behind it. On the cottage was a sign: "For Sale."   The sentiment underneath was:

> *"Peace on Earth, Good Will Toward Men;*
>   *Heh! Heh!"*

A New Year's card, with "Greetings" embossed at the top, read:

> *"If I don't see you in 1933*
>   *1934 will be soon enough for me."*

As soon as this fad caught on, the pendulum swung the other way.   The sentiments, beginning with the mildly abusive, gradually became actually vicious.

We find one, dated 1938, which says:

> *"This Christmas Eve I want you to know,*
>   *That if you don't leave $50,000 in Box 115 before*
>   *New Year's, I'll sell your letters, you crook, you."*

Another, in a wreath of mistletoe, bore the following explicit legend:

> *"Watch Your Wife."*

It was naturally but a step from these to downright obscene vituperation, and at this point, the reform societies stepped in.   A campaign was carried on throughout the country, which, unlike other re-

This was followed by a period of wide-spread bootlegging.

form campaigns, had the backing of a majority of the public. It was but the work of a year or so to induce the necessary two-thirds of the state legislatures to consent to an amendment to the constitution forbidding the manufacture and sale of Christmas cards. Naturally this was followed by a period of widespread bootlegging, but it was half-heartedly supported and soon collapsed.

All of which is merely a historical summary of what has been done in the past, preliminary to launching a campaign against the sale and manufacture of all Christmas presents, with the exception of toys. What our fathers did, we can do.

THE HENNA DECADE

What May Happen to Our Age When Thomas Beer
Catches Up to It

I

THEY put William Anderson in jail and Suzanne Lenglen tottered into the club-house with a heart-attack.

There was a pistol shot in 1922 and across silver screens from Hollywood to Lynn, Massachusetts, a resentful wraith barred attachable curls snuggling on movie lapels. "William D. Taylor has been killed," a young detective announced to his lavender mother at their California supper. And his mother smiled, for she was to hear Marion Talley before nervous wreckers dragged to earth the old Metropolitan, like avid vultures of architectural progress.

On the same border of the Pacific a blue-eyed foreman said, "Not guilty," and Roscoe Arbuckle walked out into obese freedom, cleansed with hyssop by two words from a drowsy jurist on a stool by his predecessor's desk.

2

A little boy, stooping on Central Park West, pressed cracked knuckles into creole mud and snapped roseate marbles in what passed for straight lines, while across the country in Dayton men slid against turbid waters and the National Cash Register served corporate coffee to clammy survivors. The little boy's knuckle-pressing ceased, like young leaves which refuse to burn. His father raised brown glove to lift soft fedora. "Put away your marbles," he said to the little boy, "Warren Harding has been nominated."

3

Through easy October the short French statesman in silk gloves forgot the late war in onion soup for breakfast. A very large peanut crackled in the Southern fist of Irvin Cobb and his bearded companion hailed a brown-and-white taxi. Together they swept the folio-studded Brentano's, discussing Twenty-third Street. The clerk smiled. His father had been mayor of Seattle. Would Twenty-third Street ever reach to Seattle? But Cobb had lost the large peanut and his bearded companion had lost his garter, and they left Brentano's to stand in dual

proximity watching the slightly paralytic progress
of a Number 8 Fifth Avenue bus. In the distance,
the verdant blob of Thorley's hung like a mossy
acorn—green sin on a purple republic.

4

Milt Gross stood talking with Ring Lardner and
another on the steps of the American Indian Museum. He had under his arm a bulbous bundle and
this dropped incontinently to the granite pedestal as
he shrugged his shoulders. "A peckage skelps," he
said. "Heendian skelps, witt blad." Lardner raised
a thermal eyebrow. "What of it?" he asked, and in
Chicago two young Jewish psychopathics drew up
to the curb in a Dodge looking for someone to give
a ride to. That night the Alabama delegation in
the steaming reaches of Madison Square Garden
threw twenty-five dogged votes for Oscar Under-
wood.

5

Standing, occasionally sitting, Lutitia lay in the
window seat of the Colony Club. . . . A blonde
reticence sat beside her. In the right hand of the
blonde reticence swirled a cup of tea. In her left,
a copy of November's *American Mercury*. From

its greenish covers H. L. Mencken spoke impatiently of the native *Americanus,* while George Nathan dug sadistic pins into American colleagues. Herbert Parrish disparaged the American God and words of bile were Leland H. Jenks's dole for the American Constitution and its interpreters. Fiction jetted from between these cynical rocks with gloomy disclosures of American small-town unpleasantries. Yes, Lutitia, or rather. . . .

So while Irving Berlin, a wispy figure fingering the black notes on a piano in West 46th Street, sang "Not for just a year, but always," the tug-boat, crazily bearing Mayor Hylan's Welcoming Committee, pugged to greet, with beaver boisterousness, the New Year, a rough beard swinging low over rhinestone studs.

A PLAN TO STABILIZE THE FRANC

TO the Members of the Paris Bourse (of whom it has been said, "Bourse Will Be Bourse"), Monsieur Poincare, and Fellow Guests:

I have been asked by a deputation from your delightful country to present a plan for stabilizing the franc. I feel in this connection like the three men who found themselves in a row-boat in the middle of the ocean. One was a Frenchman, one an Irishman, and one a Scotchman.

But, seriously, the problem of the franc is a vital one. And I know of no better way to handle it than the way in which we, in my household, have handled the problem of the American dollar, an even more vital problem to us, as you may well imagine. There are, at this writing, approximately twenty-five francs to each American dollar. There are also, to each American dollar, thirty-one hungry mouths. Three times six is eighteen and one to carry, six times seven is forty-two and one is forty-three and four to carry, giving a result of four hundred and sixty-one. . . . No, that can't be right. . . . Well, anyway, the life of one American dollar has been estimated at one-third that of a sugar lozenge under a faucet. This estimate gives the dollar the breaks.

Now, it was only through the most rigid household economy that we were able to stabilize the dollar in our family. Several of the older and more infirm members of the family died from under-nourishment and exposure, being unable to fight for the food or bed-clothing. But that is the Law of the Tribe, that the weaker shall give way to the stronger and those with protective coloring survive the assaults of the predatory land animals and the constant action of the tides. "Easy come, easy go," is what the old folks must remember.

Our first move toward putting our household on a gold basis was to make out a budget, and that is what you dear people of France must do, too. It is much simpler for a nation to go on a budget than for a private family, because a nation never uses real money anyway. A nation says, "Here are twenty million francs," or "Give me a hundred million dollars' worth of chips," and, if you push right up close to the counter and ask to *see* it, what do you find? A couple of theater-ticket stubs, a right-hand glove, and a piece of paper saying, "I.O.U. $100,000,000. . . . A. Mellon." There probably isn't $125 in actual cash in the whole United States Treasury at this very minute. And $45 of that belongs by rights to me, on account of the Govern-

Then hell breaks loose—telephone calls, registered letters, night sweats.

ment having disallowed my deduction for hotel expenses in my 1925 income tax. I'll get that back yet, you wait and see. The big bullies!

This system of dealing in dream-dollars, which seems to be the special prerogative of governments and large corporations, is called "Credit," and a pretty how-do-you-do it is, too. "Credit," as applied to you and me, means that we have until the fifteenth of the month to dig up the actual gold ore with which to pay our bills. But for a large corporation or a nation it means that, so long as the Treasurer can sign his name, they are on Easy Street. I sign a check, in a kidding way, and give it to Altmeyer's Meat Market. And what does Altmeyer do? Right away *he presents it at my bank!* And then hell breaks loose. Telephone-calls, registered letters, night-sweats—you'd think the whole world had gone money-mad. And I have to go and get a printing-press and *print* him his money in half a day.

But let Mr. Mellon sign a check for a billion dollars and no one even looks at the signature to see if it is genuine. It is folded up and put in the vest-pocket and never touched again for years. Is it ever presented for payment? Oh, no! Mr. Mellon signed it, never mind the money! You'd think Mr. Mellon was Richard Dix or Button Gwinnett. I could get pretty sore about the whole thing and so could you, if you had any spunk about you.

Now, in our family, there are four people, exclusive of the servant (who is lame). We have only three really to figure on, however, as the baby works.

In France, there are of course more people than that, but none nicer. It has been estimated that in each French sock there are fifteen thousand francs. In the southern provinces, where they don't wear socks, the money is stored away in the peasants' cheeks, or in hollow trees. This is going to make it hard to keep exact accounts because you can't tell how much you have on hand. But nothing is worth while unless you have to work for it, which is one of the least true things that ever was said. So what I would advise would be for every French peasant to get a little pocket note-book (the J. C. Hall Co. of Providence, R. I., sell a neat little set for a dollar, a book for each month) and keep a strict personal account of everything spent—and, what is more important, everything received.

For instance, let us take a typical French shopkeeper (and wouldn't I *like* to take one, and push him into the Somme!) named Jaques Duquesne. If we could get him to keep a personal account-book, marking down so much for *tabac,* so much for *vin,* so much for *lavabo,* and then, on the opposite page, received so much from sale to American tourist, so much from non-sale to American tourist, etc., etc., then the government officials would have a record of his financial status not one word of which could be deciphered.

But personal accounts are the only solution of the French situation, just as they were the only solution to our family crisis. My own personal account book is a joy to behold, especially if you are in the mood for a good laugh. Sometimes I get to laughing so that I can't jot down the items. "Car-fare" I put down, and I haven't ridden in a street-car since I used to go to dancing-school. Another good item is "Personal Improvement." You'd be surprised at what you can crowd into Personal Improvement. If you are anything like me practically anything you do to yourself would be an improvement. My Personal Improvement account is going to run into thousands of dollars a year, and I don't begrudge a cent of it.

To summarize then:

1. The franc is the monetary unit of France.
2. The franc is not so stable.
3. Verbs ending in *aître* retain the circumflex on the *i* whenever it is followed by *t*.
4. And how are *you?*

SEX IS OUT

ACCORDING to Dr. Max Hartmann (I used to have a dentist named Dr. Hartmann, but he was a dentist) there is no such thing as absolute sex. If 60% of your cells are masculine, you rate as a male. If 60% are feminine, you sit with the girls. All combinations are possible up to 99 and 1, but the 100 percenter in either sex is a myth. Dr. Hartmann says so.

This is going to be a big surprise to a lot of people. If the Government should ever take it into its head to make public lists of sex-percentages, as it now does income taxes, whole communities would be upset and perhaps "topsy-turvy" would not be too strong a word for what things would be.

We are concerned in this course, however, merely with the effect of this negation of sex on the drama. It looks from where we are sitting (G-112-113) like the death blow to the Living Theater in this country. And in France—well, it will simply mean that they can't give even Punch and Judy shows. What would be the fun in sitting through a scene like the following?

(The scene isn't quite set yet; so the orchestra will play the overture over again.)

ROGER: Ever since that night I met you at the dance, my male percentage has been increasing. I used to register 65%. Yesterday in Liggetts I took a test and it was eighty-one.

MARY: You had your heavier overcoat on.

ROGER: Please, dear, this is no time for joking. I never was more serious in all my life. And that means only one thing. Haven't you—aren't you—do you register just the same as you did?

MARY (*looking at her finger-nails*): No. I have gone up seven points. But I thought it was because I had cut down on my starches.

ROGER: Starches nothing! Can't you see, dear? Don't you understand what it all means?

MARY (*pulling away*): Why am I letting you talk to me like this? We mustn't. Fred will be home at any minute.

ROGER: Fred! Hah! I suppose you know what his last test was? I suppose he told you?

MARY: Why—er—no. That is—of course he did. Fred tells me everything.

ROGER: Well, then, I suppose you know that when he was examined for life insurance last week they found that his masculine cells totaled up to forty-seven and that included his American Legion button, too.

MARY: Fred? Forty-seven? Why, it isn't possible. Why, only yesterday—

ROGER: Never mind that! Figures don't lie. The best that Fred can ever be to you from now on is a sister.

MARY: This is all so sudden. I must have time to think. Fred my sister! It seems incredible!

ROGER: Don't you see, Mary dear, what the percentages tell us? (*Song Cue*)

You and I Total Up to a Hundred

Oh, Love brings a message of roses,
And Love a sweet litany tells,
Of the girls I have known, and the girls who have blown,
And their respective number of cells.

Cho.

There was Alice who rated a cool sixty-two,
She wore knickers and called me her "matey,"
There was Betty so true, with her large eyes of blue,
On a clear day she registered eighty.
There was Norma, my queen, who gave seventeen,
As her quota of masculine units,
But my heart it now yearns, on the latest returns,
(*Spoken:* Ninety-seven, ninety-eight, ninety-nine!)
For M-A-R-Y, my sweet Winona.

You can see for yourself, there is going to be no fun in figuring out sex on the back of an envelope. We might as well give the whole thing up and go in for hockey.

UNCLE EDITH'S GHOST STORY

"**T**ELL us a ghost story, Uncle Edith," cried all the children late Christmas afternoon when everyone was cross and sweaty.

"Very well, then," said Uncle Edith, "it isn't much of a ghost story, but you will take it—and like it," he added, cheerfully. "And if I hear any whispering while it is going on, I will seize the luckless offender and baste him one.

"Well, to begin, my father was a poor wood-chopper, and we lived in a charcoal-burner's hut in the middle of a large, dark forest."

"That is the beginning of a fairy story, you big sap," cried little Dolly, a fat, disagreeable child who never should have been born, "and what we wanted was a *ghost* story."

"To be sure," cried Uncle Edith, "what a stupid old woopid I was. The ghost story begins as follows:

"It was late in November when my friend Warrington came up to me in the club one night and said: 'Craige, old man, I want you to come down to my place in Whoopshire for the week-end. There is greffle shooting to be done and grouse no end. What do you say?'

"I had been working hard that week, and the prospect pleased. And so it was that the 3:40 out of Charing Cross found Warrington and me on our way into Whoopshire, loaded down with guns, plenty of flints, and two of the most beautiful snootfuls ever accumulated in Merrie England.

"It was getting dark when we reached Breeming Downs, where Warrington's place was, and as we drove up the shadowy path to the door, I felt Warrington's hand on my arm.

" 'Cut that out!' I ordered, peremptorily. 'What is this I'm getting into?'

" 'Sh-h-h!" he replied, and his grip tightened. With one sock I knocked him clean across the seat. There are some things which I simply will not stand for.

"He gathered himself together and spoke. 'I'm sorry,' he said. 'I was a bit unnerved. You see, there is a shadow against the pane in the guest room window.'

" 'Well, what of it?' I asked. It was my turn to look astonished.

"Warrington lowered his voice. 'Whenever there is a shadow against the windowpane as I drive up with a guest, that guest is found dead in bed the next morning—dead from fright,' he added, significantly.

"I looked up at the window toward which he was pointing. There, silhouetted against the glass, was the shadow of a gigantic man. I say, 'a man,' but it was more the figure of a large weasel except for a fringe of dark-red clappers that it wore suspended from its beak."

"How do you know they were dark red," asked little Tom-Tit, "if it was the shadow you saw?"

"You shut your face," replied Uncle Edith. "I could hardly control my astonishment at the sight of this thing, it was so astonishing. 'That is in my room?' I asked Warrington.

"'Yes,' he replied, 'I am afraid that it is.'

"I said nothing, but got out of the automobile and collected my bags. 'Come on,' I announced cheerfully, 'I'm going up and beard Mr. Ghost in his den.'

"So up the dark, winding stairway we went into the resounding corridors of the old seventeenth-century house, pausing only when we came to the door which Warrington indicated as being the door to my room. I knocked.

"There was a piercing scream from within as we pushed the door open. But when we entered, we found the room empty. We searched high and low, but could find no sign of the man with the shadow. Neither could we discover the source of the terrible scream, although the echo of it was still ringing in our ears.

" 'I guess it was nothing,' said Warrington, cheerfully. 'Perhaps the wind in the trees,' he added.

" 'But the shadow on the pane?' I asked.

"He pointed to a fancily carved piece of guest soap on the washstand. 'The light was behind that,' he said, 'and from outside it looked like a man.'

" 'To be sure,' I said, but I could see that Warrington was as white as a sheet.

" 'Is there anything that you need?' he asked. 'Breakfast is at nine—if you're lucky,' he added, jokingly.

" 'I think that I have everything,' I said. 'I will do a little reading before going to sleep, and perhaps count my laundry. . . . But stay,' I called him back, 'you might leave that revolver which I see sticking out of your hip pocket. I may need it more than you will.'

"He slapped me on the back and handed me the revolver as I had asked. 'Don't blow into the barrel,' he giggled, nervously.

" 'How many people have died of fright in this room?' I asked, turning over the leaves of a copy of *Town and Country*.

" 'Seven,' he replied. 'Four men and three women.'

" 'When was the last one here?'

" 'Last night,' he said.

" 'I wonder if I might have a glass of hot water with my breakfast,' I said. 'It warms your stomach.'

" 'Doesn't it though?' he agreed, and was gone.

"Very carefully I unpacked my bag and got into bed. I placed the revolver on the table by my pillow. Then I began reading.

"Suddenly the door to the closet at the farther end of the room opened slowly. It was in the shadows and so I could not make out whether there was a figure or not. But nothing appeared. The door shut again, however, and I could hear footfalls coming across the soft carpet toward my bed. A chair which lay between me and the closet was upset as if by an unseen shin, and, simultaneously, the window was slammed shut and the shade pulled down. I looked, and there, against the shade, as if thrown from the *outside*, was the same shadow that we had seen as we came up the drive that afternoon."

"I have to go to the bathroom," said little Roger, aged six, at this point.

"Well, go ahead," said Uncle Edith. "You know where it is."

"I don't want to go alone," whined Roger.

"Go with Roger, Arthur," commanded Uncle Edith, "and bring me a glass of water when you come back."

"And whatever was this horrible thing that was in your room, Uncle Edith?" asked the rest of the children in unison when Roger and Arthur had left the room.

"I can't tell you that," replied Uncle Edith, "for I packed my bag and got the 9:40 back to town."

"That is the lousiest ghost story I have ever heard," said Peterkin.

And they all agreed with him.

FASCINATING CRIMES

III. *The Missing Floor*

IT has often been pointed out that murderers are given to revisiting the scenes of their crimes. The case of Edny Pastelle is the only one on record where the scene of the crime revisited the murderer.

Edny Pastelle was a Basque elevator woman who ran one of the first elevators installed in the old Fifth Avenue Hotel, which stood at the corner of Twenty-third Street and Fifth Avenue, New York City. The elevator was of the surrey type, and was pushed from floor to floor by the operator, who was underneath climbing on a ladder. It was Mlle. Pastelle's daily task to hoist such personages as Chauncey M. Depew, Boss Tweed and Harriet Beecher Stowe up to their rooms in the Fifth Avenue Hotel. In fact, she is said to have been Miss Stowe's model for *Uncle Tom* in the novel of that name (with the word "Cabin" added to it).

In the evenings, when Edny Pastelle was not on duty, she carried Punch and Judy shows about town for whoever wanted them. As not many people

Edny Pastelle and Max Sorgossen in the gallery of human fiends and their victims.
—*Courtesy of John Held, Jr., and Life.*

wanted them, Edny's evenings were pretty much her own.

The evening of July 7, 1891, however, is on record as being not Edny's, but Max Sorgossen's.

Max Sorgossen worked in the Eden Musée, which was situated on Twenty-third Street just below the Fifth Avenue Hotel. His job was to put fresh cuffs on the wax figure of Chester A. Arthur in the Presidential Group. At five o'clock every afternoon he also took "Ajeeb," the mechanical chess player, out in the back yard for his exercise.

At five-thirty on the afternoon in question Max Sorgossen had just knocked off work and was strolling up Twenty-third Street in search of diversion. In the back of his mind was an idea that perhaps he might find another mechanical chess player for "Ajeeb" and a girl for himself and that the four of them might go down to Coney Island for the evening, as the weather was warm. As he passed the service entrance of the Fifth Avenue Hotel he met Edny Pastelle, who was likewise calling it a day. (She called it a *jour*, but that is the Basque of it.)

Edny and Max had known each other in finishing school, and so there seemed no impropriety in his speaking to her and asking her if she knew of a mechanical chess player for "Ajeeb" and if she would look with favor on an evening at Coney.

The two were seen entering a restaurant on Twenty-first Street to talk it over at 6:10. At 9:20 the next morning guests of the hotel, on trying to descend in the elevator, found it stuck between the first and third floors. When the car was finally dislodged, it was found to contain the body of Max Sorgossen. Furthermore, *the second floor, where the elevator should have stopped, was gone!*

Edny was arrested and the trial took place in the Court of Domestic Relations, since she was a domestic and there had evidently been relations, albeit unfriendly. The prosecuting attorney was a young lawyer named William T. Jerome, later William Travers Jerome. Following is a transcript of the cross-examination:

Q. What did you do after Sorgossen spoke to you on Twenty-third Street?

A. Pardon.

Q. What did you do after Sorgossen spoke to you on Twenty-third Street?

A. Plenty.

Q. Very good, Mr. Bones. And now tell me, why *is* a man with a silk hat on like Mary Queen of Scots?

A. What Scots?

Q. I'm asking *you.*

A. Animal, vegetable or mineral?

Q. Mineral.

A. The tidy on the back of that chair?

Q. No.

A. Cyrus W. Field?

Q. Give up?

A. Three spades.

Q. Double three spades.

At this point, counsel for the defense objected and the case was thrown out into a higher court, where Edny Pastelle was acquitted, or whatever you call it.

It was some thirty years later that the missing second floor of the old Fifth Avenue Hotel was discovered. A workman laying wagers on the sixteenth floor of the Fifth Avenue Building (erected on the site of the old Fifth Avenue Hotel) came across a floor which was neither the fifteenth, sixteenth nor seventeenth. The police were called in and, after several weeks of investigation and grilling, it was identified as the missing floor of the old hotel, the floor at which the little romance of Edny Pastelle had come to such an abrupt end. How it came to be on the sixteenth floor of the Fifth Avenue Building nobody knows. Perhaps Max Sorgossen could tell.

THE END OF THE SEASON

The William K. Vanderbilt mansion at Fifty-second Street and Fifth Avenue is, according to report, not to be torn down, but will be transported bodily to Long Island where it will be re-erected as a country home. The same fate is also reported to await the Cornelius Vanderbilt "château" at Fifty-seventh Street and Fifth Avenue which was sold last Spring for $7,100,000. Both mansions are, it is said, to be moved to Long Island and re-assembled by purchasers as yet unnamed.

—*News Item.*

SCENE

FIFTH Avenue between Fifty-second and Fifty-seventh Streets 3 a. m.

CHARACTERS

Mrs. Cornelius Vanderbilt's House.
Mrs. William K. Vanderbilt's House.

MRS. W. K.'s HOUSE: You-hoo!

MRS. CORNELIUS' HOUSE: You-hoo!

MRS. W. K.'s HOUSE: Are you awake?

MRS. C.'s HOUSE: Am I awake? I should say I am. We're moving down to the country tomorrow, you know.

MRS. W. K.'S HOUSE: We move down next week. How are you going down?

MRS. C.'S HOUSE: The Herman W. Oberholzer Wrecking Company, I think—if it's pleasant. The men said they would be here at seven. *Imagine!* The front steps are going down first; so there will be something there when we get there. The little towers are crazy to go down with the front steps, but I don't think I'll let them. I think they ought to stay and go down with the rest of the house. You're all going down together, aren't you?

MRS. W. K.'S HOUSE: Oh, I suppose so. I dread the whole thing and will be glad when it's over. We've had all those impossible people tramping through the house all week—charity, you know. Some days it just seemed as if I couldn't stand it. One man actually wanted to take a bath in the marble tub! My dear, I was *furious!* I think that when we do get to the country, I'll just go to bed and stay there.

MRS. C.'S HOUSE: Why don't you hurry up and come down with us tomorrow? The Oberholzer people are awfully nice and I'm sure there'd be room.

MRS. W. K.'S HOUSE: Oh, I don't know. I'm so tired I just can't think.

MRS. C.'S HOUSE: My dear, you could do it just

as easily as not. Just throw together the things you'll need—the Blashfield murals and the Caen stair-case—and have them ready at seven-thirty. Then, just as soon as we are all on the truck, I'll tell the Oberholzer men to come right over and get you and we can all go down together.

Mrs. W. K.'s House: Oh, dear, I've half a mind to do it; I do so want to get out of the city. Somehow I've been awfully depressed about things lately. New York isn't what it used to be. And then the selling of the lot and everything, and all these big business buildings coming into the neighborhood. A thirty-three story one here, you know.

Mrs. C.'s House: My dear, what do you think of *us!* A forty-two story *hotel,* if you please! We got rather used to the Plaza, but I'm glad that I sha'n't be here to see this new thing.

Mrs. W. K.'s House: Do you know, I think I'll just *tear* and get ready to go down with you in the morning. We have practically no front-steps, you know, and we can just sort of camp out down there until the roof and other things come down. Seven-thirty, you say?

Mrs. C.'s House: That's what the wrecking people said, I suppose that means eight or half-past. We'll have to eat luncheon on the way. We'll have plenty of chicken for you.

MRS. W. K.'s HOUSE: My dear, don't be silly. I'll bring the sandwiches, and perhaps when they tear the cellar up they may find enough champagne for just the two of us.

MRS. C.'s HOUSE: That will be *divine!* Seven-thirty, then.

MRS. W. K.'s HOUSE: Good night, my dear. And don't forget, I'm bringing the sandwiches!

EXAM TIME

WHAT ought to be the last word in our national craze for examinations and tests is found in the announcement of an aged man in North Carolina that he is ready to take the "Charlie Ross Test."

"The Charlie Ross Test" seems to have for its object the examination of the candidate to see whether or not he is the Charlie Ross who was kidnaped, as a little boy, from his home in Germantown, Pa., in 1873. The successful candidate is to receive an embossed certificate with the name "Charlie Ross" in Old English type at the top. He is also allowed to say, "I am Charlie Ross," when introducing himself to people.

Candidates in the Charlie Ross Test are given two hours in which to complete the examination, and a choice of seven questions out of ten. Question No. 4, however ("Are you white or black?"), must be answered, as the Charlie Ross who was kidnaped was known to have been white.

Mr. Julius Dellinger, the present contestant, has been cramming for the test for over six months, and feels fairly confident that he will pass with flying colors. A question of ruling came up last week, when it was discovered that Mr. Dellinger had been tutoring on the side with a man supposed to have been the original Charlie Ross's uncle, but it was decided to allow this provided that the candidate does not take notes into the examination-room with him.

"What will you do if you win?" Mr. Dellinger was asked.

"I will be just the happiest man in the world," was the reply. "First of all, I will have stationery made with 'C. R.' on it, and then I will look up all my new relatives in the Ross family and perhaps visit them for a while."

"When you have passed the Charlie Ross Test, do you expect to take the Ambrose Bierce Test?" the reporter asked.

"I looked into the Ambrose Bierce Test before I decided on the Charlie Ross one," Mr. Dellinger said, "but as Bierce was quite well on in years when he disappeared in Mexico, it would be rather a tough examination to take. So many people knew what Bierce looked like, and then, too, there would always be the possibility that I might *not* be Bierce after all. It would be very humiliating to get up before the Board of Regents and discover that you were

Charlie Ross when you were taking the Ambrose Bierce examination, or vice versa."

"Had you ever thought that perhaps you might be the Man with the Iron Mask?" Mr. Dellinger was asked.

"Well, that would hardly be possible," he said with a smile, "as the Man with the Iron Mask lived in the seventeenth century and spoke French. I speak no French. Still," he added with a touch of wistfulness, "I might learn."

"Aside from the language," the reporter suggested, "it ought to be an easier test than either the Ross or Bierce one, for no one knows what the Man with the Iron Mask looked like."

Mr. Dellinger thought for a minute. Then a look of determination came into his eyes. "I'll send for a set of last year's examination papers tomorrow," he said. And into his bearing there crept something of the grand manner, a slightly imperious gesture with the hand, a courtly toss to the head. For the Man with the Iron Mask was said by some to have been the son of Cardinal Mazarin and Anne of Austria.

With a low bow the reporter withdrew.

THROWING BACK THE EUROPEAN
OFFENSIVE

THIS is probably the hardest time of year for
for those of us who didn't go to Europe last
summer. It was bad enough when the others were
packing and outlining their trips for you. It was
pretty bad when the postcards from Lausanne and
Venice began coming in. But now, in the fall, when
the travelers are returning with their Marco Polo
travelogs, now is when we must be brave and give a
cheer for the early frost.

There are several ways to combat this menace of
returning travelers. The one that I have found most
effective is based on the old football theory that a
strong offense is the best defense. I rush them right
off their feet, before they can get started.

In carrying out this system, it is well to remember
that very few travelers know anything more about
the places they have visited than the names of one
hotel, two points of interest, and perhaps one street.
You can bluff them into insensibility by making up
a name and asking them if they saw that when they
were in Florence. My whole strategy is based on

my ability to make up names. You can do it, too, with practice.

Thus, let us say that I am confronted by Mrs. Reetaly who has just returned from a frantic tour of Spain, southern France, and the Ritz Hotel, Paris. You are inextricably cornered with her at a tea, or beer night, or something. Following is a transcript of the conversation. (Note the gathering power of my offense.)

Mrs. R.: Well, we have just returned from Europe, and everything seems so strange here. I simply can't get used to our money.

Mr. B.: I never see enough of it to get used to it myself. (*Just a pleasantry.*)

Mrs. R.: When we were in Madrid, I just gave up trying to figure out the Spanish money. You see, they have *pesetas* and—

Mr. B.: A very easy way to remember Spanish money is to count ten *segradas* to one *mesa,* ten *mesas* to one *rintilla* and twenty *rintillas* to one *peseta.*

Mrs. R.: Oh, you have been to Spain? Did you go to Toledo?

Mr. B.: Well, of course, Toledo is just the beginning. You pushed on to Mastilejo, of course?

Mrs. R.: Why—er—no. We were in quite a hurry to get to Granada and—

Mr. B.: You didn't see Mastilejo? That's too

bad. Mastilejo is Toledo multiplied by a hundred.
Such mountains! Such coloring! Leaving Mastilejo, one ascends by easy stages to the ridge behind
the town from which is obtained an incomparable

"Unless you have seen Tuna, you haven't seen Spain."

view of the entire Bobadilla Valley. It was here
that, in 1476, the Moors—

MRS. R.: The Moorish relics in Granada—

MR. B.: The Moorish relics in Granada are like
something you buy from Sears-Roebuck compared to
the remains in Tuna. You saw Tuna, of course?

MRS. R.: Well, no (*lying her head off*), we were
going there, but Harry thought that it would just be
repeating what—

Mr. B.: The biggest mistake of your life, Mrs. Reetaly, the biggest mistake of your life! Unless you have seen Tuna, you haven't seen Spain.

Mrs. R.: But Carcassonne—

Mr. B.: Ah, Carcassonne! Now you're talking! Did you ever see anything to beat that old diamond mill in the *Vielle Ville?* Would they let you go through it when you were there?

Mrs. R.: Why, I don't think that we saw any old diamond mill. We saw an old—

Mr. B.: I know what you're going to say! You saw the old wheat sifter. Isn't that fascinating? Did you talk with the old courier there?

Mrs. R.: Why, I don't remember—

Mr. B.: And the hole in the wall where Louis the Neurotic escaped from the Saracens?

Mrs. R.: Yes, wasn't that—? (*Very weak.*)

Mr. B.: And the stream where they found the sword and buckler of the Man with the Iron Abdomen?

Mrs. R. (*edging away*): Yes, indeed.

Mr. B.: And old Vastelles? You visited Vastelles, surely? . . . Mrs. Reetaly, come back here, please! I just love talking over these dear places with someone who has just been there. . . . May I call on you some day soon and we'll just have a feast of reminiscence? . . . Thank you. How about tomorrow?

And from that day to this, I am never bothered by Mrs. Reetaly's European trip, and you needn't be, either, if you will only study the above plan carefully.

The other method is based on just the opposite theory—that of no offense, or defense, at all. It is known as "dumb submission," and should be tried only by very phlegmatic people who can deaden their sensibilities so that they don't even hear the first ten minutes of the traveler's harangue. The idea is to let them proceed at will for a time and then give unmistakable evidence of not having heard a word they have said. Let us say that Mr. Thwomly has accosted me on the train.

Mr. T.: It certainly seems funny to be riding in trains like this again. We have been all summer in France, you know, and those French trains are all divided up into compartments. You get into a compartment—*compartimon,* they call them—and there you are with three or five other people, all cooped up together. On the way from Paris to Marseilles we had a funny experience. I was sitting next to a Frenchman who was getting off at Lyons—Lyons is about half way between Paris and Marseilles—and he was dozing when we got in. So I—

Mr. B.: Did you get to France at all when you were away?

Mr. T.: This was in *France* that I'm telling you

about.   On the way from Paris to Marseilles.   We
got into a railway carriage—

"Did you get to France at all when you were away?"

Mr. B.: The railway carriages there aren't like
ours here, are they?   I've seen pictures of them, and
they seem to be more like compartments of some
sort.

Mr. T. (*a little discouraged*): That was a French railway carriage I was just describing to you. I sat next to a man—

Mr. B.: A Frenchman?

Mr. T.: Sure, a Frenchman. That's the *point*.

Mr. B.: Oh, I see.

Mr. T.: Well, the Frenchman was asleep, and when we got in I stumbled over his feet. So he woke up and said something in French, which I couldn't understand, and I excused myself in English, which *he* couldn't understand, but I saw by his ticket that he was going only as far as Lyons—

Mr. B.: You were across the border into France, then?

Mr. T. (*giving the whole thing up as a bad job*): And what did *you* do this summer?

Whichever way you pick to defend yourself against the assaults of people who want to tell you about Europe, don't forget that it was I who told you how. I'm going to Europe myself next year, and if you try to pull either of these systems on *me* when I get back, I will recognize them at once, and it will just go all the harder with you. But, of course, *I* will have something to tell that will be worth hearing.

AN INTERVIEW WITH VICE-PRESIDENT DAWES

INTERVIEWING Vice-Presidents is always a ticklish business, unless you happen to find one who isn't ticklish.

So I took General Dawes into my confidence right at the start.

"General Dawes," I said, "what is your feeling about the Senate?"

"You mean the Roman Senate, do you not?" asked the grizzled warrior.

"Well, yes, now that you speak of it," I replied. Here was a chance to have some fun at the expense of Catiline.

"The Senate is all right," said General Dawes. "It is the tribunes of the people that cause all the trouble. They and the lictors."

"How would you lictor have a glass of beer?" I asked the Vice-President.

Well, that got us to giggling, as you may very well imagine. First I would hit him, and then he would hit me.

"If the Senate rules were to be changed, so that for 'quorum' it should read 'jorum,' what would you think?" I asked him, spitting out two teeth (good ones, too).

" 'Jorum' instead of 'quorum'?" he asked, stalling for time. "What would I think?"

"You heard me, Mr. Vice-President," I retorted.

"I should say, suh—" he began.

"I didn't know that you were from the South," I interrupted.

"I'm not. That was just something caught in my throat."

At this point, General Dawes looked out the window. "Where are we?" he asked, peering into the darkness. "Is this New Haven we are coming into, porter?"

But the porter was just as much puzzled as General Dawes was, being a Southern Pacific porter on his first trip on the N. Y., N. H. & H. R. R.

"I could tell with a bit of litmus paper," he said.

Quickly I clapped my hand over General Dawes' mouth.

"Do you ever wonder, Mr. Vice-President," I asked him, "just what life is all about?"

"*Do* I?" said General Dawes from behind my palm. "That's all I ever wonder about."

"Wasn't it Voltaire who asked *'Que suis-je, ou suis-je, ou vais-je, et d'ou suis-je tiré?'* "

"That all sounds very silly," retorted the General in a rage. "And besides, there should be an accent over all those 'u's'."

"The General did not have his nap today," I explained to the conductor. "He is cross."

"This is my street anyway," said the Vice-President, hopping up and getting into his middy-blouse. And, without a word, he was gone.

THE *LIFE* POLAR EXPEDITION

*E*N *route with "Life's" Bicycle Expedition to the North Pole.—May 17.*

We are now just between Woodlawn and Mt. Vernon, at a point where there seems to be some sort of road-digging going on. This means that we shall have to sit down and wait for them to finish, or else go back and take a roundabout route. We are just a little discouraged.

"Chief," Lieut.-Commander Connelly said to me as we were pedalling through Morrisania (168th Street), "do you ever have any doubts about our catching up with the others—Amundsen and Byrd, I mean?"

I felt a strange little chill creep around my heart. Was this mutiny?

"Have you heard any of the men talking?" I asked, without looking at him.

"Well, no, not exactly," he replied, "but Ensign Thermaline asked me yesterday how long I figured out that it would be before we sighted one of the other expeditions."

"You can tell Ensign Thermaline," I said, "that if he will keep his feet pedalling 'round and 'round just as fast as he can and maintain his balance, the rest of us will do the same."

Lieut.-Commander Connelly looked at me with tears in his eyes. "Aye, aye, sir," was all that he said, but it spoke volumes.

From Mott Haven, where we spent the night, we have pedalled due north over the Grand Concourse, stopping only once at a repair shop to get a new thumb-piece for Ensign Thermaline's bell. Ensign Thermaline had been using the bell almost constantly since leaving 57th Street, being one of the most cautious pilots in the expedition.

A peculiarity of the country which we all have noticed since crossing over the Harlem River is the rows upon rows of large apartment houses which have sprung up along the route. At first none of us spoke of it, but finally Lieut.-Commander Connelly could keep his thoughts to himself no longer. "Have you noticed the large number of apartment houses along the way?" he asked. We all admitted that we had.

In front of one of these apartment houses an interesting sight met our eyes. A little boy was seen riding along in what looked like a very small automobile and it was in effect really an automobile except that it was propelled by the little boy's feet, which were in direct contact with the sidewalk. Some members of the expedition were in favor of stopping and getting the little boy to join, but wiser counsel prevailed and we decided that it would take him too long to get his winter things packed and that we ought not to incur any more delays than we should run into in the natural course of events. "He would have been cute, though," said Lieut.-Commander Connelly wistfully.

Just the other side of Williamsbridge we ran into an obstacle which for a while threatened to hold us up indefinitely. Right in our path we came to a high wall surrounding a reservoir. We sent Ensign Thermaline up to take soundings and he returned, making a long face, and reporting that the reservoir was practically ten feet deep.

"What a place to build a reservoir anyway!" I said, and the other joined me in my disgust.

Fording the darned thing being out of the question, we decided that it would be better to take one of the roads which seemed to lead around it. We chose the one to the left because left is Lieut.-Commander Connelly's favorite direction. And Dame Fortune was with us in our choice, for it led, after a while, right into the Bronx River Parkway, which was *just* where we wanted to be. Had we taken the road to the right, there is no telling where we should have ended up.*

It was in passing Woodlawn Cemetery that we got into the discussion which is still raging as we sit by the roadside before Mt. Vernon. The sight of the miles and miles of monuments in Woodlawn depressed Lieut.-Commander Connelly and set him thinking.

"Man's span is *so* short," he said, drawing up alongside my "bike" (as we call our wheels). "Man's span is so short that it seems hardly worth all the fuss and pother of trying, doesn't it?" he whispered.

"I think that word is 'bother,' " I said.

"Which word?" he asked.

"The word you called 'pother,' " I replied, a little cruelly, I am afraid.

"Are you *sure?*" he asked.

"As sure as one can be of anything in this old world," I said.

"That's just it," the lieutenant-commander returned, "what *can* one be sure of? We are born, grow up, make our little plans—and what sad, brave little plans they are, too—and then just as we think we are succeeding"—the young explorer stopped

* The right road also leads to the Bronx River Parkway.—
EDITOR.

and looked at the rows of tombstones on our left.

"I know, Lieutenant-Commander," I said, sympathetically. "You don't have to say it."

And so we rode on in silence, until we reached this sort of digging-up they are doing in the road. Then I said: "Oh, the devil!" And at this rather pat climax to a discussion on philosophy, we both laughed.

But if we are held up very long here it will be no laughing matter, for in the papers we read that Amundsen is already on his way to the Pole from Spitzbergen.

(*The brave boys of the "Life" Polar Expedition are pedalling furiously in a northerly direction and expect to reach Mt. Vernon any day now. Another despatch from Commander Benchley will appear next week.*)

A GHOST STORY

(As Sherwood Anderson Would Write It If He Weren't Prevented)

I

DAVID PERK sat on the edge of his bed. It was nearly midnight and in a few minutes the ghost would come. The ghost would come, all right, all right. Why not? Milt Neevis had seen it here in this very room, and Milt got drunk every Thursday night and rolled in the bran-mash they had fixed for the horses out in Rob McCarver's barn. And Milt knew women, too. When Spring came to Panis Junction, and the soft smell of honeysuckle drifted into town over Ernest Tamson's tannery down by the tracks, Milt used to sneak out at eleven o'clock every night and go in swimming alone in the Women's Public Baths. Naked. Milt knew women all right. Lordy!

And Milt Neevis had told David Perk that at midnight the ghost would be sure to come. And what's more, it might be a female ghost, Milt said. Male and female. Hot dickety-dog!

142

2

David Perk was sitting on the edge of his bed
waiting for the ghost. Why should he—David Perk
—be afraid? Why should anyone be afraid? Why
should you be afraid? Why should I be afraid?
Sex was sex, wasn't it? That night in Chicago.
Why had he left Ella? Ella had been his first wife
and every Friday night she used to bake potatoes
and cut them open to put butter in them. David
had liked to see her cut open the baked potatoes.
Perhaps it hurt them to be cut open. Why not?
Potatoes had sex, just the same as you and me or
old Milt Neevis rolling in the bran-mash out in Rob
McCarver's barn. Male potatoes. Female potatoes. Cut them open and put butter in them. And
paprika. Ella had cut them open and put butter in
them that night back in Chicago. And David had
left her. Not because she did that. David had
liked that. It had made him feel all queer all over.
Lordy! Ella would never understand how it made
him feel. So he had left her. Male potatoes in
the same dish with female potatoes. Milt Neevis
swimming alone naked in the Women's Public Baths
on a Spring night. Slicky-slicky!

3

David Perk sitting on the edge of his bed waiting for the ghost. Perhaps a girl ghost. He was a man, wasn't he? Secretary Stanton of Lincoln's cabinet had been a man, hadn't he? Why Stanton? Well, why not Stanton? He, David Perk, had never seen Stanton, had he? Nor G. A. Henty. Nor Cyrus W. Field. All men, weren't they? And what were men made for if not for women?

"Hill-dill, come over the hill,
Or else I'll catch you standing still."

That night in Detroit. When he had left Irma. Irma had been his second wife. Irma had large bones and cried easily. One night in the Spring she and David had gone out into the fields and pulled up all the grass. A mare and a stallion pulling up grass in the fields and chewing it. They had chewed grass all night. Big sensation. Grass between your teeth. Green, sharp grass. Big male moon in the sky looking for its mate. Little female stars skipping about looking for their mates. Never finding them. David never finding anyone. Twenty-three! Skidoo!

4

That night in Boston when David had met

Theresa. Theresa was his third wife. The State House dome in the moonlight. Niggers singing on the Common. Niggers who had been freed. Irishmen singing on the Common. Sailors with girls on their laps on the benches. Spooning. Tremont Street. Boylston Street. Trolley cars. English sparrows with Spring in their veins. Men and women. Boys and girls. Male babies and female babies. Sex! America!

And here was he, David Perk, sitting—all hot and bothered—on the edge of his bed waiting for the ghost to come. And old Milt Neevis down in Rob McCarver's barn rolling in the bran-mash.

5

Downstairs Edith was asleep. Edith was David Perk's fourth wife. Edith slept on her right side with the right arm stretched out behind her and her left hand under her cheek. And after that— what? After *what* what? What did it matter what? Here was the ghost. The ghost that Milt Neevis had told him about. And Milt had said it might be a female!

David felt all queer. He felt as he had felt that night in Toronto when he had left Marian, his fifth wife. "All alone by the telephone waiting for a

ring, a ting-a-ling." Things hadn't gone right—for
him and Marian—not right at all.

> *"Higgledy-piggledy, my black hen.*
> *She lays eggs for gentlemen."*

Eggs for gentlemen, eh? Lord, what a time!
But what was a fellow to do? What had she been
thinking about? What had he—David—been
thinking about? Chinks jabbering in their laundry.
Chinks jabbering out in front of their laundry.
The War. The Red Cross. The Fifth Liberty
Loan. Was he—David—afraid? Was he—or was
she—jealous of her? Not by a damn sight. Well,
he and Irma had certainly messed things up. And
he smiled to himself. Would the ghost know?
Would she understand what Irma hadn't understood? What Marian hadn't understood? What
Edith—downstairs sleeping this very minute with
her right arm stretched out behind her—wasn't understanding? How come?

6

It was Spring outside and the warm breeze over
the lilac bushes carried the smell of Ernest Tamson's
tannery to David. Did the ghost smell it too?
"Come in." David was out of bed now, standing

beside the ghost. She was a woman all right. And
David was a man. God's man. Flames in her
eyes—deep red flames—deep blue flames. The old
oaken bucket. The iron-bound bucket. The moss-
covered bucket. Heigh-ho! Old Black Joè!

David was packing his grip. His two military
brushes. One male. The other female. Male and
female created He them. Why be ashamed of it?
The ghost was looking at David with a queer look
in her eyes. She knows what's what, old man. Sure
thing. She wants me to go with her. Why not?
Male and Female created He them. And the evening and the morning were the sixth day. "And
'twas from Aunt Dinah's quilting party, I was seeing Nelly home."

7

David Perk and the girl ghost were leaving the
house. He felt her close to him. It was! It
wasn't! It was! He knew that she was thinking
the long, long thoughts of a woman. And he—
David—was thinking the long, long thoughts of a
man. They were across Nalbro Harris' backyard
now. Now they were on the train for Chicago. Mr.
and Mrs. David Perk. And back in the gray house
Edith was sleeping with her right arm stretched out
behind her and her left hand under her cheek. On
her right side. Well, toodle-oo!

DISCOVERING WEBER AND FIELDS

If There Had Been Erudite Criticism in the Nineties

FROM the lowly precincts of the music halls has arisen a new pair of pragmatists. The names that appear on the bills are Weber and Fields, but the hands are the hands of William James. And so and so and so and so.

The method of these zanies is eclectic. From Zeno the Stoic they have taken the doctrine of "six-times-six-is-thirty-six." From Anaxagoras the theory that the Whole is less than any of its parts. From Francis Bacon the denial of Truth as a substantive. From L. G. B. three dozen woolen stockings and a crate of oranges.

Take for example the scene where *Mike* and *Meyer* are discussing occupations (in itself pure dialectics):

MEYER: Vot are you doing?
MIKE: Voiking in a nut factory.
MEYER: Doing vot?
MIKE: Nutting.
MEYER: Sure—but vot are you *doing?*
MIKE: Nutting.
MEYER: I know, but vot voik are you doing?

MIKE: Nutting, I tole you.

MEYER (*poking his finger in Mike's eye*): Ou-u-u-u, how I lofe you!

Here we have the new philosophy of the subconscious, the stirrings of a new American humor which derives from the modern German school of *Merkwürdigkeit,* or *Es-giebt-also-es-ist.* In the American mind is being born, through the medium of the music hall, a consciousness of national social satire which bids fair to revolutionize thought on this side of the Atlantic. Could a better example be found than the following dialogue between these two super-clowns in their latest show:

MIKE (*referring to off-stage noises*): A soldier has been shot.

MEYER: Vere vos he shot?

MIKE: In de eggcitement!

Here, in these words, lies America. The America of today, with its flaring gas lights, its thundering cable cars, the clatter of its hansoms, and the deafening whistle of its peanut stands. The young, vibrant spirit of America, locked in the message of two clowns! And, with the coming of jazz, twenty years from now, we shall see the full expression of the young nation's strivings toward the Greater Smooch.

WATER FOOTBALL

Suggestions to the Rules Committee for Making Use of Rain

WHATEVER it is that the football rules committee does during that week in the spring that it spends in New York (and you can't tell me that a group of healthy men can stay in a New York hotel room all the time and think of nothing but football, football, football) it certainly makes no provision for rain on the day of a big game. And anyone who has sat through four two-hour periods in a downpour will tell you that football, as it is played today, is essentially a fair-weather sport.

I had a cousin who went to the Harvard-Yale game last year and contracted gelatin-trouble, owing to the sizing in his fur coat having soaked through into his spine and gone the rounds of his entire system. He sat in a large puddle (one of the largest in the Yale Bowl, he tells me, and you know what a big place the Yale Bowl is) and along about six o'clock, on the way home in the machine, he felt a queer sort of spinal disintegration. "As if I were going to pieces," is the way he expressed it. He thought nothing of it until his arms and legs began to come off and then he went somewhere and lay down. Whatever it was that finally became of him, the point is that watching football in the rain is no darned fun and the least that the rules committee can do is to make some regulations covering a situation that so frequently exists.

For instance, when it is found that the field is going to be knee-deep in mud and water, there ought to be some way of changing the nature of the game entirely, so that the very elements which would, under the old rules, work toward a spoiling of the game, might be turned into favorable factors for all concerned.

Thus we might have a play (to be called "left half around the sandbar") in which, at the signal, the left halfback takes the ball from the quarter, tosses it into a dory, shoves off, and rows around right end. His interference, also in dories, could ward off tacklers by splashing water in their faces, use of the oars as clubs to be called illegal. To meet this play, it would be the function of the defensive backs to row through and, if possible, force the man with the ball in his boat to row onto a sandbar or else create such a wash that it upsets him.

Or, there might be an entirely different ball used during a rain storm—a large, red rubber ball such as some nuisance always has at the beach in the summer. This could be tossed back and forth, the players screaming with excitement the while, until one side or the other gets tired. With this type of ball, a very neat trick play could be utilized, the "U-56, or concealed ball play" in which the quarterback, immediately on receiving the pass, would shove the ball under the surface of the water, sit on it, and paddle himself around left end or through left tackle, if a hole could be opened up for him. The fun here would be for the defense to drown the runner.

Of course, the rain is not always sufficiently heavy to make the water deep enough for the two plays outlined above. Sometimes it merely drizzles and there is nothing but mud on the field. This would call for an entirely new list of plays. Under these conditions, the old Carlisle Indian trick could be revived, each of the backs scooping up an armful of mud and running with it, the defense being unable to tell in which armful the ball is hidden. Or, as an alternate play, the backfield could daub their faces with mud to look like a negro quartette and could start humming old plantation melodies. Then, while the defense stopped and listened, enchanted, the right end could pick up the leather and slide down the field with it.

The big spectacular play, however, for a muddy

day is the "sappers' wedge" or "East Side subway." In this trick, the linemen throw up breastworks of mud in front of the line of scrimmage. When the ball is put into play, the backs burrow down into the soft ground and tunnel themselves under the line, digging out on the other side for a gain of perhaps five yards. This play can be used effectively when within five yards of the goal, as the back carrying the ball has made, *ipso facto*, a touchdown.

This outline of aquatic football has, however, not taken the spectators into account. Who ever does? But there they are, millions and millions of them, and something must be done for *them* on a rainy day.

Since there is always someone in front of you who has an umbrella up, you might as well give up any idea you may have had of watching the game. Don't torture yourself by trying to peek around the umbrella, catching sight of the beginning of a play and never knowing until you hear the cheering whether or not it succeeded. In this way lies madness. Just give up trying to spy on the field maneuvers and get your neighbors to enter into a few little games with you to pass the time away.

There is, for example, the game of "Neck Cisterns." In this game, all the people sitting in a row open out the collars of their coats in the back, sitting hunched forward so as to make the opening as big as possible. The idea is to see who can catch the most rain water down the back of the neck. Drippings from an umbrella are not allowed. The water must come directly down and into the collar. The winner is the one whose collar runs over first.

This may seem like a very simple game to play, and one dependent entirely on the capacity of the coat of the contestant. This is not so. A great deal of skill can be brought into playing it by adjusting the angle of the body to meet the angle of the rain at a point where the maximum amount of water will drive into the collar. An old hand at "Neck Cisterns" can fill his coat up to overflowing before a beginner has got even his shoulder blades wet.

Another similar game is that of "Brimming." The players in this turn the brims of their hats up so as to catch the rain water. At a given signal, the brims are suddenly turned down and the heads thrust forward, the idea being to project the deluge of water as far out as possible. The one hitting the person farthest in front wins and is the champion "brimmer" of the section. During the final period of the football game, the champion "brimmers" from each section meet and play off the finals.

Of course, one of the chief features of watching a contest in the rain is the wet seat. You hop up in your excitement at seeing the boys pull off a forward

The one hitting the person farthest in front wins.

pass (which is grounded) and, by the time you have got around to sitting down again, the place which you have been keeping dry up until the forward pass is now a tiny lily pond with swan boats in it. Into this you sink back exhausted from your cheering, and in it you sit for the rest of the game while, starting from the pond as a base, a series of chills race up your spine to a spot directly behind your ears, where they break ranks.

One of the most interesting by-products of watching a football game in the rain occurred in Lawrence, Massachusetts, in 1919. It had rained all during the first three periods of the game and everyone was sitting in individual pools, giving the matter no more thought. Several hundred of them had been fighting a brave fight against the cold and damp by means of that greatest little cold and damp fighter of them all, the pocket flask, and these brothers didn't even *know* that they were sitting in water. They knew that they were sitting pretty and it didn't make any difference to them where. Suddenly, at the beginning of the fourth period, the weather changed and grew much colder. There was a great deal of time out and dull playing, and no one felt called upon to hop up for quite some time. As a matter of fact, the game ended with the ball in mid-field and a lot of

substitutes running in to get their letter. When the
whistle blew, the fans started to get up to go home,

. . . found they were frozen to the stands.

but found that they were frozen to the stands. The
entire Lawrence fire department came with axes and
worked until eleven that night chopping the people

out. A couple of old grads, who had very poor seats down in the corner behind the goal posts, were overlooked and had to stay there until spring.

In order to avoid a recurrence of this unfortunate accident, and in general to keep the seats dry, it has been suggested that the rules committee make it illegal for any spectator to jump to his feet during a game. This would apply even when two rival rooters started a fist fight in the stand. Coincident with the passage of this rule, similar prohibitions might be put on a man's falling when dropped out of a window, and on the earth's rotating on its axis.

MORE SONGS FOR MELLER

AS Señorita Raquel Meller sings entirely in Spanish, it is again explained, the management prints little synopses of the songs on the program, telling what each is all about and why she is behaving the way she is. They make delightful reading during those periods when Señorita Meller is changing mantillas, and, in case she should run out of songs before she runs out of mantillas, we offer a few new synopses for her repertoire.

(1) ¿VOY BIEN?
(AM I GOING IN THE RIGHT DIRECTION?)

When the acorns begin dropping in Spain there is an old legend that for every acorn which drops there is a baby born in Valencia. This is so silly that no one pays any attention to it now, not even the game-keeper's daughter, who would pay attention to anything. She goes from house to house, ringing doorbells and then running away. She hopes that some day she will ring the right doorbell and will trip and fall, so that Prince Charming will catch her.

159

So far, no one has even come to the door. Poor
Pepita! if that is her name.

(2) Camisetas de Flanela
(flannel vests)

Princess Rosamonda goes nightly to the Puerta
del Sol to see if the early morning edition of the
papers is out yet. If it isn't she hangs around humming to herself. If it is, she hangs around humming
just the same. One night she encounters a young
matador who is returning from dancing school. The
finches are singing and there is Love in the air.
Princess Rosamonda ends up in the Police Station.

(3) La Guia
(the time-table)

It is the day of the bull fight in Madrid. Everyone is cock-eyed. The bull has slipped out by the
back entrance to the arena and has gone home, dis-
gusted. Nobody notices that the bull has gone except Nina, a peasant girl who has come to town
that day to sell her father. She looks with horror
at the place in the Royal Box where the bull ought
to be sitting and sees there instead her algebra
teacher whom she had told that she was staying at

home on account of a sick headache. You can imagine her feelings!

(4) No Puedo Comer Eso
(I can not eat that!)

A merry song of the Alhambra—of the Alhambra in the moonlight—of a girl who danced over the wall and sprained her ankle. Lititia is the ward of grouchy old Pampino, President of the First National Banco. She has never been allowed further away than the edge of the piazza because she teases people so. Her lover has come to see her and finds that she is fast asleep. He considers that for once he has the breaks, and tiptoes away without waking her up. Along about eleven o'clock she awakes, and is sore as all get-out.

(5) La Lavandera
(The laundryman)

A coquette, pretending to be very angry, bites off the hand of her lover up to the wrist. Ah, naughty Cirinda! Such antics! However does she think she can do her lessons if she gives up all her time to love-making? But Cirinda does not care. Heedless, heedless Cirinda!

(6) Abra Vd. Esa Ventana
(open that window)

The lament of a mother whose oldest son is too young to vote. She walks the streets singing: "My son can not vote! My son is not old enough!" There seems to be nothing that can be done about it.

FASCINATING CRIMES

IV. The Lynn Horse-Car Murders

EARLY in the morning of August 7th, 1896, a laborer named George Raccid, while passing the old street-car barns at Fleeming and Main Streets, Lynn, Massachusetts, noticed a crowd of conductors and drivers (horse-cars were all the rage in 1896) standing about a car in the doorway to the barn. Mr. Raccid was too hurried to stop and see what the excitement was, and so it was not until the following Wednesday, when the bi-weekly paper came out, that he learned that a murder had been committed in the car-barn. And at this point, Mr. Raccid drops out of our story.

The murder in question was a particularly odd one. In the first place, it was the victim who did the killing. And in the second, the killing occurred in a horse-car, an odd conveyance at best. And finally, the murderer had sought to conceal his handiwork by cramming his victim into the little stove in the middle of the car, a feat practically impossible without the aid of scissors and a good eye for snipping.

The horse-car in which the murder occurred was one of the older types, even for a horse-car. It was known in the trade as one of the "chummy roadster" models and was operated by one man only. This man drove the horses, stoked the fire, and collected the fares. He also held the flooring of the car together with one foot braced against a "master" plank. On his day off he read quite a lot.

The murder car and its driver, Swelf Yoffsen.
—*Courtesy of John Held, Jr., and Life.*

The driver of the murder-car was named Swelf Yoffsen, a Swedish murder-car driver. He had come to this country four years before, but, not liking it here, had returned to Sweden. It is not known how he happened to be back in Lynn at this late date.

If we have neglected to state the name of the

victim thus far, it is because nobody seemed able to identify him. Some said that he was Charlie Ross, who had disappeared shortly before. Others (the witty ones) said it was Lon Chaney. A vote taken among all those present designated him as the one least likely to succeed.

An interesting feature of this crime was that it was the sixth of a series of similar crimes, all of which had occurred in Swelf Yoffsen's horse-car. In the other five cases, the victims had been found inadequately packed in the stove at the end of the run, but as Yoffsen, on being questioned, had denied all knowledge of how they got there, the matter had been dropped. After the discovery of the sixth murder, however, Yoffsen was held on a technical charge of homicide.

The trial was one of the social events of the Lynn Mi-Careme season. Yoffsen, on the stand, admitted that the victim was a passenger in his car; in fact, that he was the only passenger. He had got on at the end of the line and had tried to induce Yoffsen to keep on going in the same direction, even though the tracks stopped there. He wanted to see a man in Maine, he had said. But Yoffsen, according to his own story, had refused and had turned his horses around and started for Lynn again. The next he saw of him, people were trying to get him out of the stove. It was Yoffsen's theory that the man, in an attempt to get warm, had tried to crowd his way into the stove and had smothered. On being reminded that the affair took place during a very hot week in August, Yoffsen said that no matter how hot it got during the day in Lynn, the nights were always cool.

Attorney Hammis, for the State, traced the movements of Yoffsen on the morning of the murder and said that they checked up with his movements on the occasions of the five other murders. He showed that Yoffsen, on each occasion, had stopped the horse-car at a particularly lonely spot and asked the occupants if they minded making a little detour, as there was a bad stretch of track ahead. He had then driven his horses across a cornfield and up a nearby hill on the top of which, in the midst of a clump of bayberry bushes, stood a deserted house. He pointed out that on four out of the six occasions Yoffsen had driven his horses right into the house and asked the passengers (when there were any, other than his victim) if they would step into the front room for a few minutes, giving them some magazines to read while they waited. According to the testimony of seven of these passengers, after about fifteen minutes Yoffsen had appeared and yelled "All aboard!" in a cheery voice and everyone had piled back into the horse-car and away they had gone, over the cornfield and down the hill to Lynn. It was noted that on each occasion, one of the passengers was missing, and that, oddly enough, this very passenger was always the one to be found in the stove on the way back.

It was the State's contention that Yoffsen killed his victims for their insurance, *which is double when the deceased has met his death in a common carrier*.

On April 14th, the ninth day of the trial, the jury went out and shortly after asked for a drink of water. After eighteen hours of deliberation they returned with a verdict of guilty, but added that, as it was not sure whether Yoffsen had actually killed his victims *in* the car or had killed them outside and *then* stuffed them in the stove, he was not entitled to the double insurance.

When they went to inform Yoffsen of the verdict, he was nowhere to be found.

THE *LIFE* POLAR EXPEDITION

*E*N route with "Life's" Bicycle Polar Expedition.—May 24.

We chose this route northward, through Mt. Vernon, Tuckahoe and Scarsdale, because we figured out that it might be pleasant to stop off at my house in Scarsdale for maybe a bite to eat, or, in case there was not time for that, at any rate to let the boys see our bicycles. But I guess now that we would have done better to take the Hudson River road.

We reached Scarsdale late yesterday afternoon, intending to put in at my side-yard, get a drink of cool water and perhaps a pocketful of Rosa's cookies, show my two boys how the gyro-balancer works, and then push on to White Plains for the night. The cool-water-and-cookies part of the plan worked out to the dot, but in demonstrating the gyro-balancer to the boys we ran into a snag which has held us up for an entire day.

It was really due to the kind-heartedness of Lieut.-Commander Connelly that the whole thing happened. He insisted on removing his gyro-balancer from the frame of his "bike" in order to show Nathaniel, my older boy, just how it worked, and, as he did so, he laid the loose nuts on a piece of paper on the ground. Robert, my younger boy (who is only six and so mustn't be blamed too much), claims that he didn't go near the paper or the nuts. And he probably doesn't realize that he did. But one of the nuts was found over a nail on a boat that he was working on a few feet away, and the other had disappeared completely.

A search was immediately instituted which covered every square inch of the lawn and extended into the street—those things roll so. But when darkness came we were no nearer to finding it than we had been at the beginning, and it was necessary to telephone back into New York for an extra nut, which they said they would send out the first thing in the morning. It is now 4:17 in the afternoon and the man hasn't come yet. We are very discouraged.

It was while we were searching for the nut that a neighbor came up and asked us if we had heard anything about the Byrd expedition's having flown over the Pole. I got him aside out of earshot of the other men and asked him if he was sure. He said no, but that he had seen a cartoon in some paper which seemed to have reference to a successful flight by Byrd. I, however, laughed his fears away

and went back to the search.   Even if Byrd *does*
beat us to it, his victory will have been by flying-
machine, while ours will be by bicycle—two entirely
different things.

The trip from Mt. Vernon to Scarsdale was one
of great beauty and was accomplished without a
mishap. The route led along the Bronx River Parkway, through woods and across streams, which made
up in a way for the rough time we had in the traffic
in New York City.

While passing through Tuckahoe, Lieut.-Com-
mander Connelly saw a scarlet tanager perched on a
bush overhanging the stream.   Thinking that it
might be interesting to have it for our collection of
flora and fauna which we are making for the
Museum, we dismounted and crept up very quietly
beside it, thinking to bag it before it could collect
its wits. But it heard us coming and flew away.

There is a particularly odd family of ferns which
grows along the bank of the Bronx River, and, ferns
not being as agile as birds, we were able to pick
great quantities of it.   I wish that some of my
readers could tell me what the name of it is.   It is
green, like other ferns, but it seems to have a sort
of flower which looks like a carnation.   The blossom
was still in bud and so we were unable to tell exactly
what it does look like, but I should say that a carna-

tion would just about fit it. Any naturalist who happens to have run across this fern, and who knows what it is, would relieve our minds considerably if he, or she, would write to the *Life* Polar Expedition, General Delivery, White Plains, N. Y., and tell us. Just a regular fern, with a carnation blossom.

We are now going out into the side-yard again with a flashlight to take another look for the missing nut, as evidently the man from town isn't going to bring out that extra one today, and we *must* get started early tomorrow morning.

Every cloud, they say, has a silver lining, and, as a result of our being held up here in Scarsdale like this, we have been able to have some of Rosa's excellent baked-beans. I find it almost impossible to get *real* New England baked-beans in this region, unless you tell someone just how they should be done. In the first place, it must be a California pea-bean that is used, and these should be put to soak the night before and then baked in a slow fire all the next day. If we had got away when we expected, the beans would not have been ready. So perhaps we were a little harsh with Bobbie.

AN INTERVIEW WITH THE COUNTESS KAROLYI

AN interview with Countess Karolyi was very difficult to get, as she is not allowed to enter this country and I am not allowed to leave it. So we met at the drug store on the corner.

The Countess being Hungarian, it seemed that the least I could do would be to conduct the interview in her native tongue. It certainly wasn't the *best* I could do.

"*Hogy szercted americat?*" I began, as a feeler. It wasn't much, as feelers go, but I am not very strong.

"*Közönöm nomigon nagyon,*" she replied, blushing prettily. I had not looked for this frankness. I glanced out over the blue Mediterranean, obviously waiting for her to break the silence. I had not long to wait.

"*Asz önök epülitegi igon maghsak,*" she said, so low that I could hardly hear her. It was like a bombshell.

I wheeled and confronted her.

"*Gindolja hogy a Ni holgye ink szójeck talán?*"

The situation demanded it. I have no apologies to offer.

Fortunately for the interview, the bell in the monastery tolled eleven at just this moment. There was one extra stroke—for the war tax.

"Hánz ora?" I asked, more for something to say than anything else.

Countess Karolyi glanced over her shoulder apprehensively. I had evidently confused her.

"Tisz peresel mult öt," was all that she could reply. But it was enough. I had fainted.

"Do you mind if we speak English from now on?" she said when I had opened my eyes. "You speak Hungarian so fast that it is difficult to follow you."

I smiled. "Look!" I said, pointing to the courtyard below. They were changing the guard, a ceremony which consisted of putting a false beard and blue glasses on the watchman. It certainly changed him, except that his nose gave him away.

"Maqyen szcretez Te enzom?" I asked. It was a silly thing to say, but it seemed pat at the moment. Now I realize that it was mike.

Her reply was characteristic. *"Nom magyen,"* she said and hid her face.

We reached home at eight o'clock, tired but happy, and all agreed that it had been the most interesting hike the Club had taken thus far.

THE BOYS' CAMP BUSINESS

THERE seems to be an idea prevalent among parents that a good way to solve the summer problem for the boy is to send him to a boys' camp. At any rate, the idea seems to be prevalent in the advertising pages of the magazines.

If all the summer camps for boys and girls turn out the sterling citizens-in-embryo that they claim to do, the future of this country is as safe as if it were in the hands of a governing board consisting of the Twelve Apostles. From the folders and advertisements, we learn that "Camp Womagansett—in the foothills of the White Mountains" sends yearly into the world a bevy of "strong, manly boys, ready for the duties of citizenship and equipped to face life with a clear eye and a keen mind." It doesn't say anything about their digestions, but I suppose they are in tiptop shape, too.

The outlook for the next generation of mothers is no less dazzling. "Camp Wawilla for Girls," we learn, pays particular attention to the spiritual development of Tomorrow's Women and compared to the civic activities of the majority of alumnæ of Wawilla, those of Florence Nightingale or Frances

Holding you under water until you are as good as drowned.

Willard would have to be listed under the head of "Junior Girls' Work."

Now this is all very splendid, and it is comforting to think that when every boy and girl goes to Womagansett or Wawilla there will be no more Younger Generation problem and probably no crime waves worth mentioning. But there are several other features that go hand in hand with sending the boy to camp which I would like to take up from the parents' point of view, if I may. I will limit myself to twenty minutes.

In the first place, when your boy comes home from camp he is what is known in the circular as "manly and independent." This means that when you go swimming with him he pushes you off the raft and jumps on your shoulders, holding you under water until you are as good as drowned—better, in fact. Before he went to camp, you used to take a kindly interest in his swimming and tell him to "take your time, take it easy," with a feeling of superiority which, while it may have had no foundation in your own natatorial prowess, nevertheless was one of the few points of pride left to you in your obese middle-age. After watching one of those brown heroes in one-piece suits and rubber helmets dive off a tower and swim under water to the raft and back, there was a sort of balm in being able to turn to your son

"Now watch Daddy. See? Hands like this, bend your
knees. See?"

and show him how to do the crawl stroke, even though you yourself weren't one of the seven foremost crawl experts in the country. You could do it better than your son could, and that was something.

It was also very comforting to be able to stand on the springboard and say: "Now watch Daddy. See? Hands like this, bend your knees. See?" The fact that such exhibitions usually culminated in your landing heavily on the area bounded by the knees and the chest was embarrassing, perhaps, but at that you weren't quite so bad as the boy when he tried the same thing.

But after a summer at camp, the "manly, independent" boy comes back and makes you look like Horace Greeley in his later years. "Do this one, Dad!" he says, turning a double flip off the springboard and cutting into the water like a knife blade. If you try it, you sprain your back. If you don't try it, your self-respect and prestige are shattered. The best thing to do is not to hear him. You can do this by disappearing under the surface every time it looks as if he were going to pull a new one. After a while, however, this ruse gets you pretty soggy and waterlogged and you might better just go in and get dressed as rapidly as possible.

The worst phase of this new-found "independence" is the romping instinct that seems to be de-

veloped to a high state of obnoxiousness at all boys'
camps. I went to camp when I was a boy, but I
don't remember being as unpleasant about my fun
as boys today seem to be. I have done many mean
things in my time. I have tortured flies and kicked
crutches out from under cripples' arms. But I have
never, so help me, Confucius, pushed anybody off
a raft or come up behind anyone in the water and
jumped up on his shoulders. And I don't think that
Lincoln ever did, either.

There is evidently a course in raft pushing and
back jumping in boys' camps today. Those photographs that you see in the camp advertisements, if
you examine them closely, will disclose, in nine cases
out of ten, a lot of boys pushing each other off rafts.
You can't see the ones who are jumping on others'
shoulders, as they are under water. But I want to
serve notice right now that the next boy who pushes
me off a raft when I am not looking, or tries to play
leapfrog over me in ten feet of water, is going to be
made practically useless as Tomorrow's Citizen, and
I am going to do it myself, too. If it happens to be
my own son, it will just make the affair the sadder.

Another thing that these manly boys learn at camp
is a savage habit of getting up at sunrise. The normal, healthy boy should be a very late sleeper. Who
does not remember in his own normal, healthy boy-

hood having to be called three, four, or even five
times in the morning before it seemed sensible to get
up? One of the happiest memories of childhood is
that of the maternal voice calling up from down-

You'd be surprised at the sound two bicycle wheels can make
on a gravel path.

stairs, fading away into silence, and the realization
that it would be possibly fifteen minutes before it
called again.

All this is denied to the boy who goes to a summer
camp. When he comes home, he is so steeped in the
pernicious practice of early rising that he can't shake
it off. Along about six o'clock in the morning he

begins dropping shoes and fixing up a new stand for the radio in his room. Then he goes out into the back yard and practices tennis shots up against the house. Then he runs over a few whistling arrangements of popular songs and rides his bicycle up and down the gravel path. You would be surprised at the sound two bicycle wheels can make on a gravel path at six-thirty in the morning. A forest fire might make the same crackling sound, but you probably wouldn't be having a forest fire out in your yard at six-thirty in the morning. Not if you had any sense, you wouldn't.

Just what the boys do at camp when they get up at six is a mystery. They seem to have some sort of setting-up exercises and a swim—more pushing each other off the raft—but they could do that by getting up at eight and still have a good long day ahead of them. I never knew anyone yet who got up at six who did anything more useful between that time and breakfast than banging a tennis ball up against the side of the house, waiting for the civilized members of the party to get up. We have to do enough waiting in this life without getting up early to wait for breakfast.

Next summer I have a good mind to run a boys' camp of my own. It will be on Lake Chabonagog- chabonagogchabonagungamog—yes, there is, too, in

Webster, Massachusetts—and I will call it Camp Chabonagogchabonagogchabonagungamog for Manly Boys. And by the word "manly," I will mean "like men." In other words, everyone shall sleep just as long as he wants, and when he does get up there will be no depleting "setting-up" exercises. The day will be spent just as the individual camper gosh-darned pleases. No organized "hikes"—I'd like a word on the "hike" problem some day, too—no camp spirit, no talk about Tomorrow's Manhood, and *no pushing people off rafts.*

AT LAST A SUBSTITUTE FOR SNOW

WHILE rummaging through my desk-drawer the other night I came upon a lot of old snow. I do not know how long it had been there. Possibly it was a memento of some college prank long forgotten. But it suddenly struck me what a funny thing snow is, in a way, and how little need there really is for it in the world.

And then I said to myself, "I wonder if it would not be possible to work up some sort of mock snow, a substitute which would satisfy the snow people and yet cause just as much trouble as real snow." And that, my dears, is how I came to invent "Sno."

As you know, real snow is a compound of hydrogen, oxygen, soot, and some bleaching agent. (There is a good bleaching agent who has an office in Room 476, Mechanics' Bank Building. He was formerly General Passenger Agent for the Boston and Maine, but decided that bleaching was more fun. As a matter of fact, his name is A. E. Roff, or some such thing.)

Again, as you know, real snow is formed by the passage of clouds through pockets of air which are lighter than the air itself, if such a phenomenon were possible. That is to say, these clouds (A) passing through these air-pockets (C) create a certain atmospheric condition known as a "French vacuum." This, in turn, creates a certain amount of ill-feeling, and the result is what we call "snow," or, more often, what we call "this lousy snow."

Now in figuring out what I would have to do to concoct a mock snow, it was necessary to run over in my mind the qualities of snow as we know it. What are the characteristic functions of snow?

Well, first, to block traffic. Any adequate substitute for snow must be of such a nature that it can be applied to the streets of a city in such a way as to tie up all vehicular movement for at least two days. "This," I thought, "requires distribution." Our new snow must be easily and quickly distributed to all parts of town. This will necessitate trucks, and trucks will necessitate the employment of drivers. *Now,* if the weather is cold (and what good is snow unless the weather is cold enough to make it uncomfortable?) these drivers (B) will have to have mittens. So mittens are the first thing that we must get in the way of equipment. . . . And I took a piece of paper and wrote down "Mittens." This I crossed out and in its place I wrote "Mittens" again. So far, so good.

Next, one of the chief functions of real snow is to

get up in under the cuffs to your sleeves and down inside the collar to your overcoat. Here was a

... hire boys to run along beside people to tuck the substitute in their sleeves.

tough one! How to work up something which could be placed up the sleeves and inside the overcoat-collars of pedestrians without causing them the inconvenience of stopping and helping the process. For no substitute for snow could ever be popular which called for any effort on the part of the public. The public wants all the advantages of a thing. Oh, yes! But it doesn't want to go to any trouble to get them. Oh, no! No trouble! If it is going to have snow up its sleeves and in its collars, it wants it put there while it is walking along the street, and no stopping to unbutton or roll back.

So it was evident that, if this function of snow was to be imitated, it would be necessary to hire boys to run along beside people and tuck the substitute in their sleeves and collars as they walked. One boy could perhaps tuck two hundred handsful in an afternoon, and when you figure out the number of people abroad on a good snowy afternoon, you will realize the enormous number of boys it would take to do the job. Girls would be even worse, because they would stop to talk with people.

The problem of distribution thus unsuccessfully met with, the next thing was to decide what other attribute our "Sno" should have that would give it a place in the hearts of millions of snow-lovers throughout the country. Someone suggested "wetness" and in half a second the cry had been taken up in all corners of the conference-room (for we were in conference by now), "Wetness! Wetness! Our 'Sno' must be wet!"

It was decided that the place in which we should have to simulate wetness the most was under bedroom windows. Who does not remember getting up to shut the bedroom windows and stepping into a generous assortment of snow-flakes in their prettiest form of disintegration—water? Or even into a drift 'way, 'way out in the middle of the room right where Daddy could slip in it on his way to and from the office? This is perhaps the most difficult feature of snow to imitate—this bedroom drifting, and if, in addition to getting our composition snow into bedroom windows, we could manage some appliance whereby it could be shot into the folds of whatever underclothing might be lying on the chair nearest the window, then indeed might we cry "Eureka!"

The way in which we decided on the name "Sno" for our product would make a story all in itself. The copyright laws forbid one from naming anything "Snow" or "Gold" or "Rolls-Royce," or any noun. This law was passed by some fanatics who took advantage of our boys being away at war to plunge the country into an orgy of blue laws. However, we have no other curse than to abide by the code as it stands.

We therefore decided that, by dropping the *W*,

we could make a word which would sound almost like the real word and yet evade the technical provisions of the law. Some of the backers held out for a dressier-sounding name, like "Flakies" or "Lumpps," but our advertising man, who specializes on Consumer Light Refractions, told us that the effect of a word like "Sno" on the eye of the reader would telegraph a more favorable message to his brain than that of a longer word ending in "ies" or "umpps." Look at the word "Ford," for instance. The success of the Ford product is almost entirely due to the favorable light refractions of the name on the consumer's retina.

This decided us on the trade-name "Sno" and left nothing more for us to do but work out the actual physical make-up of the product and the sort of package to put it out in. The package is also an important feature of any merchandising scheme, and it was decided that a miniature snow-show would be appropriate and rather smart for our particular article. If we could work out some way in which "Sno" could be wrapped up in a six-inch snow-shoe it would not only give the dealer something snappy to display, but would make a nice-looking package for the consumer to take home—nicer-looking than a snootful of scotch, for example. You would be surprised, however, to find how difficult it is to wrap up a unit of imitation snow in a snow-shoe, unless you put them both in a box together.

And now all that remains to divulge is the physical make-up of "Sno." That is what we are working on now.

THE NEW WING

(*Or That Sagredo Bed*)

ALTHOUGH the new wing of the Metropolitan Museum of Art ("Wing K," if that makes it any easier for you) was opened on April 5th, I have only just this week got around to inspecting it. I'm sorry.

"Wing K" has, since 1916, been empty, and, although passers-by late at night have often reported strange noises coming from its vast recesses, the Museum officials stubbornly maintain that it has been put to absolutely no use at all. This sounds a little fishy to me, however, and if those old walls could talk we might learn a little something more about where Mr. Munsey's money went. It is said that only a couple of hundred dollars remain of all the millions that he bequeathed to the Museum. Money doesn't *fly* away, you know.

At any rate, "Wing K" is full now and it takes a good twenty minutes of fast walking to see everything in it. This does not include the time taken up in getting lost or in walking through the same hall twice.

As Mr. MacGreggor got tired and cross he began sniveling.

My inspection was somewhat hampered by having Mr. Charles MacGreggor along with me. Mr. Mac-Greggor kept constantly asking to see Dr. Crippen. "I want to see Dr. Crippen," he would say, or "Where is Dr. Crippen?" I told him that the wax-works were in another wing of the Museum, but someone had told him that a replica of Dr. Crippen was to be found in "Wing K" and nothing would do but he must see it. Along toward the end, as Mr. MacGreggor got tired and cross, he began sniveling and crying, "I want to see Dr. Crippen" so loudly that an attendant put us out. So we probably missed some of the funniest parts of the exhibit. If you want me to I will go up again sometime without Mr. MacGreggor. Or maybe Dr. Crippen *is* there, after all.

The feature of the new wing is, of course, the Bedroom from the Palazzo Sagredo at Venice. The best way that I can describe it is to say that it is fully twice the size of our guest room in Scarsdale, and fifty per cent fancier. The chief point in favor of our guest room in Scarsdale is that there isn't a whole troop of people strolling through it at all hours of the day, peeking under the bed and asking questions about it. If you want to sleep after nine in the morning in Scarsdale you can do it without being made an exhibition of. My two little boys may romp into the room three or four times during the morning to show you an engine or a snake, but all that you have to do is to tell them to get the hell out or you will tell me on them.

The owner of the Palazzo Sagredo was a great cupid fancier. Over the doorway to the alcove where the bed is, there are over a dozen great, big cupids stuck on the wall, like mosquitoes in a summer hotel. They are heavy, hulking things and seem to have fulfilled no good purpose except possibly to confuse any guest who may have retired to the fancy bed with a snootful of good red Sagredo wine. To awaken from the first heavy sleep of a Venetian bun and see fifteen life-sized cupids dangling from the doorway must have been an experience to send the eighteenth century guest into a set of early eighteenth century or late seventeenth century heebes. The comic strip on the ceiling is catalogued as "Diziani's Dawn." It may very well be.

This, in a general way, covers pretty well the Bedroom from the Palazzo Sagredo. In another month the Gideons will have slipped a Bible onto the table by the bed and it will be ready for occupancy, but not by *me*, thank you.

Walking rapidly through the rest of the new wing, you come to lots of things in cases which, frankly, do *not* look very interesting. There is a bit of sculp-

ture labeled "Head of Zeus(?)" showing that even
the Museum officials don't know whom it is meant
to represent. Under the circumstances, it seems as
if they might have cheated a little and thrown a
bluff by just calling it arbitrarily "Head of Zeus"
without the question mark. Certainly no one could
have called them on it, and it would have made them
seem a little less afraid to take a chance. Suppose
that it turned out *not* to be Zeus. What is the worst
that could happen to them?

Then, too, there is "A Relief from a Roman
Sarcophagus." As we remember Roman sarcophagi,
anything would be a relief from them.

We could go on like this for page after page
making wise-cracks about the various uninteresting
features of the new wing, but perhaps you have
already got the idea. It may have been the absence
of Dr. Crippen, or it may have been a new pair of
shoes, but the truth is that we weren't *put* out of the
new wing. We *asked* an attendant how to *get* out.
And here we are.

UNCLE CALVIN'S NO-WASTE GAMES

There is a time for play as well as a time for work. But even in play it is possible to cultivate the art of well-doing. Games are useful to train the eye, the hand and the muscles, and bring the body more completely under the control of the mind. When this is done, instead of being a waste of time, play becomes a means of education.—*President Coolidge's Christmas Message to the boys and girls of the nation.*

AND now come, boys and girls, it's play-time! You have worked hard *enough* for one day, and Uncle Calvin is going to teach you some peachy games to clear the cobwebs out of those brains of yours. Play-time! Play-time!

But first of all we must remember that play in itself is a waste of time. And who remembers what we learned yesterday about Wasted Time? The boy or girl who wastes time, or anything else, is just as naughty as the boy or girl who steals, for, after all, wasting *is* stealing, isn't it? And play, just for the sake of play, is stealing time which belongs rightfully to our parents, our teachers or our country. And we don't want to be known as *thieves*, do we?

So the games which Uncle Calvin is going to teach

us are games which will do us good in one way or another. While we are playing them we shall, at the same time, be helping to make our eyes, our hands, and our minds more efficient. And, as we play, we must keep thinking: "Is this helping me? Or am I wasting time which I ought to be devoting to my lessons or my work or my country?"

The first game that we are going to play is called

EYE-SPY

This is just lots and lots of fun—and good for your eyes, too. The boys line up on one side, and the girls on the other. Now Uncle Calvin will stand over here and write on the board a lot of little teeny-weeny figures, problems in percentage, and we will see which can read them off and answer the problems the faster—the boys or the girls. Come now, boys, you don't want the girls to beat you, do you? All right . . . ready, get set . . . *go!*

Now we are going to play a dandy game called

DRY, TOM, DRY

We must remember in playing this game not to get all hot and sweaty and too excited, for it is *really* a game to train our hands. Three girls come over here to the sink, and three boys stand in a line from the sink to the table. Now each boy gets a brand new wiper and each girl a little tub full of hot water and dirty dishes. Now the game is to see which girl and her boy-partner can wash and dry her dishes first. As each dish is cleaned it is handed to the boy with the towel and when he has dried it he places it on the table. You must be very careful in passing the dishes not to drop them. Here is where the excitement comes in. For if you drop and break a plate, Uncle Calvin will lick hell out of you. . . . Now, no giggling, Walter Pearson! You don't see Uncle Calvin giggling, do you? All ready? . . . Then—*play!*

And now for our final game we have a big surprise for you. The game is called

PRINTER'S-PIE

and what do you think? You are all actually going to take part in the Government of this big country which we all love so well! We are going to play a game called "type-setting" and, when we have finished, we will find that we have not only had loads and loads of fun, but that we have saved the Government thousands and thousands of dollars. Now here is how the game is played:

Each child brings his little savings-bank to Uncle

Calvin and with what Uncle Calvin finds in there he will buy a box of type and a "galley" for each one. Then you stand in front of a high sort of desk and take a piece of paper which Uncle Calvin will give you. On this paper will be written something— different things—which your government wants to have printed. You will follow this very, very care- fully, and try and find the little pieces of type in the box to correspond with the letters in the "copy." When you find the right letter, place it in a little case which you hold in your hand until all the letters form the same words as those in your "copy." Now put these words and sentences in the "galley," or "holder" and pretty soon you will find that you have an exact duplicate *in type* of the page which Uncle Calvin has given you. Isn't that exciting! An *exact* duplicate! This page of type will then be taken from you and plates made from it and then it will be *printed* and you will see your own work in the *Congressional Record* and all the little pamphlets that your congressman sends you. Just think! Your own work in print!

And, just because you have had all this fun, your government will have been able to cut down its print- ing appropriation to almost nothing and you will have trained your eyes and your hands and your minds which will please Uncle Calvin more than he can say.

And now that we have had our play, we must scamper back to work, for, as Uncle Calvin said in his cheery Christmas message, there is a time for play as well as a time for work, and, so long as you don't *waste* time when playing, you will be able to work all the better for your parents, your schools, and your country.

THE WORLD OF GRANDPA BENCHLEY

Thinking Out Loud in the Manner of
Mr. Wells' Hero

§1

I AM eighty-nine years old, and I think I would like to write a book. I don't know—maybe I wouldn't.

§2

Eighty-nine this year, ninety next year, eighty-eight last year. That makes three years accounted for. Three into fourteen goes four times and two to carry. The Assyrians were probably the first people to evolve mathematics. I sometimes get to thinking about mathematics.

The average Englishman at the age of eighty-nine is dead—has been dead for several years. The average depth of the Caspian Sea is 3,000 feet. The average rainfall in Canada is 1.03 inches. During the Inter-Glacial Period it was 9.01 inches. Think of that—9.01 inches!

§3

All this has made me stop and think, think about
the world I live in. I sometimes wonder what it is

Grandpa Benchley.

all about—this world I mean. I am not so sure
about the next world. Sometimes I think there is

one and sometimes I think there isn't. I'll be darned if *I* can make it out.

I am not so sure about my wanting to write a book, either. But something has got to be done about this world—something explanatory, I mean. Here I am, eighty-nine years old, and I haven't explained about the world to anyone yet—that is, not to anyone in this room.

§4

It is a beautiful day outside. The sun, that luminous body 95,000,000 miles from the earth, without which we should never be able to dry hides or bake biscuits, is shining through the trees outside my window, much as it used to shine through the trees outside the cave of Neolithic Man, ten thousand years before Christ. In fact, Neolithic Man sometimes built himself houses on piles driven in the water, but this was not until almost five thousand years before Christ.

Sometimes I get to thinking about Neolithic Man. Sometimes I get to thinking about Cro-Magnon Man. Sometimes it just seems as if I should go crazy thinking about things. There are so *many* things! And I am only eighty-nine.

§5

I remember when I was a very small boy my mother used to forbid me to go out when it was raining. My mother was a very quiet woman, who never spoke unless it was to figure out how long it would take to reach the nearest star by train.

"Nipper," she would say to me on such days as the rain would prevent my going out, "Nipper, I guess you don't know that thousands of years before modern civilization there was a period known as the Pluvial or Lacustrine Age, the rain or pond period."

I remember my crying myself to sleep the first night after she told me about the Pluvial or Lacustrine Age. It seemed so long ago—and nothing to be done about it.

§6

One night my father came home with a queer light in his eyes. He said nothing during dinner, except to note, as he passed me the salt, that salt is an essential to all grain-consuming and herbivorous animals but that on a meat-diet man can do without it. "There have been bitter tribal wars," he said, "between the tribes of the Soudan for possession of the salt deposits between Fezzan and Murzuk."

"Arthur," said my mother, quietly, "remember the boys are present."

"It is time they knew," was his reply.

At last my mother, sensing that something was troubling him, said:

"Arthur, are you holding something back from me?"

He laid down his knife and fork and looked at her.

"I have just heard," he said, "that the molecule is no longer the indivisible unit that it was supposed to be."

My mother bit her lip.

"You tell me this," she said, "after all these years!"

"I have just learned it myself," replied my father. "The National Molecule Society found it out themselves only last month. The new unit is to be called the 'atom.' "

"A fine time to tell me!" said my mother, her eyes blazing. "You have known it for a month."

"I wasn't sure until just now," said my father. "I didn't want to worry you."

My mother took my brother and me by the hand. "Come, boys," she said, "we are going away."

Two days later the three of us left for the Continent. We never saw my father again.

§7

This set me to thinking about atoms. I don't think that I have it straight even now. And then, just as I was getting accustomed to the idea that molecules *could* be divided into atoms, along comes somebody a few years ago and says that you can divide atoms into electrons. And, although I was about seventy-five at the time, I went out into the park and had a good cry.

I mean, what is an old fellow going to do? No sooner does he get something all thought out than something happens to make him begin all over again. I get awfully sore sometimes.

§8

Then there is this question of putting studs in a dress-shirt. Here is the problem as I see it:

If you put the studs in *before* you put the shirt on, you muss your hair putting it on over your head. If you wait until you have the shirt on before putting in the studs, you have to put your hand up under the front of the shirt and punch them through with the other. This musses the shirt bosom nine times out of ten. Eight times out of ten, perhaps.

All right. Suppose you put the studs in first and muss your hair. Then you have to brush it again.

That is not so hard to do, except that if you put tonic on your hair before you brush it, as I do, you are quite likely to spatter drops down the bosom. And there you are, with a good big blister right where it shows—and it's 8 o'clock already.

Now here *is* a problem. I have spent hours trying to figure some way to getting around it and am no-where near the solution. I think I will go to the Riviera where it is quiet and just think and think and think.

§9

I am sitting at my window in the *Villa a Vendre* at Cagnes. If it were not for the Maritime Alps I could see Constantinople. How do you suppose the Alps got there, anyway? Some giant cataclysm of Nature I suppose. I guess it is too late to do anything about it now.

Irma is down in the garden gathering snails for dinner. Irma is cross at me because this morning, when she suggested running up to Paris for the shooting, I told her that the ancient name of Paris was Lutitia.

I get to thinking about women sometimes. From eight in the evening on. They are funny. Female characteristics differ so from male characteristics.

This was true even in the Pleistocene Age, so they tell me.

§10

Next Wednesday I am going back to thinking about God. I didn't anywhere near finish thinking about God the last time. The man came for the trunks and I had to go with him to the station.

It is quite a problem. I don't think there is any doubt about there being some Motive Power which governs the World. But I can't seem to get much beyond that. Maybe I'll begin again on that Monday. Monday is a good day to begin thinking. Your laundry is just back and everything is sort of pristine and new. I hope that, by beginning Monday, I can get everything cleaned up by Friday, for Friday I am going over to Monte Carlo.

§11

It is six years now since I began writing this book. I am almost ninety-seven. According to the statistics of the Royal Statistical Society I can't expect much longer in which to think things over.

The big thing that is worrying me now is about putting sugar on my oatmeal. I find that if I put the sugar on first and then the cream, the sugar all disappears, and I like to see it, nice and white, there

on the cereal. But if I put the cream on first and
then the sugar, it doesn't taste so good. I asked
Irma about this the other day and she told me to
shut up and go back to bed.

§12

After thinking the whole thing over, I have come
to the conclusion that I don't want to write a book
at all. When a man is ninety-seven it is high time
he was doing something else with his time besides
writing books. I guess I'll go out and roll down hill.

THE *LIFE* POLAR EXPEDITION

I

*A*T *the Hop-off of* LIFE's *Polar Expedition, Scarsdale, N. Y. (Second Lap)*—Here we are, much to our surprise, all set for the second big lap on our expedition to the North Pole by bicycle, begun last spring. Those of you with a scientific turn of mind who have followed us thus far will remember that we were held up in my home in Scarsdale by a lost nut and that, by the time we were ready to start on again, news had come of the so-called successful completion of the Byrd and Amundsen expeditions.

The positive assurance that we had been beaten in the race to the Pole, with our goal practically within pedaling distance, as you might say, was naturally very depressing. Lieutenant-Commander Connelly took the thing particularly to heart, as he had *so* wanted us to be first. We found him that afternoon in the Bronx River Parkway, kicking a tree much bigger than himself and half-sobbing, half-laughing: "Darn-darn-double-darn!" and "You old *tree*, you!"

I myself was quite disheartened but tried not to

show it to the brave boys who had come so far and had shown such splendid spirit. So I proposed that we go back to the house and sing some songs. I wish that you might have seen the will with which the rest of the crew took up my suggestion, and have heard the room ring with the sounds of "Upidee" and "Solomon Levi" when we finally got down to it. Both Lieutenant-Commander Connelly and Ensign Thermaline sang tenor.

It was Ensign Thermaline who finally spoke the words which gave us new courage to continue on our expedition in spite of the self-styled winners, Byrd and Amundsen.

"Why should we stop," he asked, toppling off the piano bench, "just because some wise-cracking aviators have flown over the Pole? Our aim was not to *fly*. It was to bicycle. That popular interest in polar expeditions has died down should mean nothing to us. That the New York *Times* will not take any more expedition articles until it uses up those it has on hand means nothing to us. We can get to the Pole and back before the George Palmer Putnam series has even been got together in book form. We can still be the first to bicycle across the Pole—and, by the Eternal, we will!"

At this we were on our feet and cheering. Rosa brought in a plate of hermits and we sat over these

until far into the night making plans for our second
dash to the Pole.

It was decided that, since the Putnam expedition
on the *Morrissey* was being written up by Mr. Putnam's little boy David, we should take my little boy
Bobby along as official yeoman and that all reports
should be written by him.   He is seven, and no one,
not even his teacher, can read his writing; so he
seemed practically ideal.

We also decided that we ought to have names for
our bicycles (like the Putnam's *Morrissey*), and
Lieutenant-Commander Connelly immediately chose
"The O'Toole" for his, and Ensign Thermaline
"Mavourneen" for his.   Mine was to be "The Ban-
shee."

The next thing to do was to buy a small bicycle
for Bobby, and, believe it or not, it took until just
this week to find one small enough.   However, Scarsdale was very pleasant during the summer and we
all were very happy and brave, and here we are
ready to start tomorrow, "rain or shine," as Lieutenant-Commander Connelly expressed it, laughing
to hide his tears.

2

*Special North Pole Correspondence from Bobby
Benchley, Juvenile Member of* LIFE'S *Bicycle Expedition.   En route to Pole.*

North White Plains, N. Y.—When we left Scarsdale on the second dash to the Pole my father told
me that he would write the account of our trip and
that I should sign my name to it, as every expedition
has to have a little boy along who writes a book
about it later.

"You write it and I sign it?" I asked him.

"That's right, Bobby," he said. "Daddy writes
it and Bobby signs it and Bobby gets all the publicity."

"Publicity me eye," was my answer. "If I sign
it, I write it. I'll take no responsibility for your
drivel. I know your stuff and I prefer to write my
own, *if* you don't mind. The rest of the school
would kid the pants off me if one of your books
came out with my name signed to it."

This angered my father and he made as if to hit
me, but I ducked and ran into the house.

"All right for you, you big bully!" I yelled out at
him. "Just for that I won't *go* on your old expedition."

This sobered him up and he agreed to let me write
my own stuff and sign it and take ten per cent. of
the royalties. If the book sells as it ought to, with
any kind of pushing at all from the publishers, I
ought to clean up enough to marry Ruthie Henshel
in the spring.

So here we are, as far as North White Plains, and very dull it has been up till now, too. We left Scarsdale at ten o'clock Wednesday morning, I on my new Demon with special coaster-brake attachment and a swell cap with a big visor on it to keep the Artic sun out of my eyes. It is my private opinion that all the Artic sun we see on this trip you could *put* in my right eye and I'd never notice it.

(*Proofreading note by Benchley, Sr.*—I *told* Bobby he ought to let me write out a rough draft for him first. You see what he has done with "Arctic." However, if he is going to be just stubborn about the thing—)

The trouble with the expedition so far is that my father and Lieut.-Commander Connelly get winded so soon. They can't pump up even a little hill without having to get off at the top and rest. We're lucky to be at North White Plains, let alone the North Pole. I began by going on ahead as fast as I could, but this just made them sore and I lost them going through Hartsdale and had to sit down by the roadside and wait for them to come up. They both got pretty fat during the summer hanging around at the base in Scarsdale, and my father especially has got to look out or he'll look something awful in another year. I told him so, too, and he told me to shut up or he'd send me away to military school.

Well, anyway, what with the old folks puffing along behind and Ensign Thermaline having to stop off in White Plains to see an old girl of his, it has taken us just four days to get this far.

Coming through White Plains, my father tried to tell me about the battle that was fought there during the Revolutionary War.

"What battle was that?" I asked.

"The Battle of White Plains, of course," he said. "What did you think it was, the Battle of Princeton, N. J.?"

"Princeton beat Harvard, didn't they?" I came back at him.

At this he made a lunge for me, and fell off his bicycle, which got me to laughing so hard I had to stop, too.

"And who won the Battle of White Plains, Father dear?" I asked him, trying to change the subject.

"The Americans did, of course," he said, brushing himself off.

"Yeah?" I said. "So the Americans won, did they? Well, that shows what *you* know about it. The British won. We had it in school only last week."

"What school?" asked my father, very sore now.

"Not Harvard, anyway," I said. "Yale beat Harvard, too."

"Yeah?" he said, getting redder and redder. "Yale beat Harvard by playing twelve men against Harvard's eleven. . . . And if you aren't a better boy, Daddy's going to send you right back to Scarsdale on the 4:10 from White Plains."

"The 4:10 doesn't stop at Scarsdale," I said. "It's an express to 125th St."

"Let's be getting on," interrupted Lieut.-Commander Connelly. "This is no way to get to the North Pole—arguing about Harvard and Yale."

So we all got on our wheels again and pushed ahead, but I think I'll drop off at Mt. Kisco and see the Barry kids. My time is worth *something*.

HOW TO START A SUPPER CLUB

YOU think that the housing problem in New York is pretty critical, don't you? Well, that just shows how much you know about it. The problem isn't how to take care of all the people who live in New York; it's how to take care of all the people who dance there. Night clubs are springing up like mushrooms (not exactly like mushrooms but near enough) and still there is a shortage. A lot of people have to go home every night without dancing. And you know what that leads to.

A man can't turn his back on a block between Fiftieth and Fifty-ninth Streets without three new supper clubs appearing before he looks back again. I left my house in Fifty-fifth Street one Wednesday morning (it was the Wednesday morning I left my house in Fifty-fifth Street) and after a hard day at the office returned Friday night to find that four stables on our block (I am a horse writing this: "Black Beauty") had been transformed into "La Vache Noire," "Sally Sobel's Cellar," "The Old Oaken Bucket," and "Club O'Hara." It has got so that you can't leave your ice box out on the back porch without someone coming along and turning it into a night club.

The process of transforming a stable or an ice box or a fair-sized umbrella closet into a supper club is pretty simple, once you get the hang of it.

First comes the coat room. This has to be the first feature on the way in, in order to be the last one on the way out, so that the coat room girl can get that last fifty-cent piece that the patron has been holding out for taxi fare. You wouldn't believe the number of cheap skates that try to sneak out with fifty cents or a dollar hidden away in their clothes. It kind of makes you lose your faith in human nature.

From the coat room you arrange a hidden step so that the guest stumbles down into what used to be the place where they kept the mops and brooms and into the arms of the head waiter. This gives the head waiter the chance to accuse the patron of being drunk and refuse him admission.

The choice of a head waiter is very important. Go down to the wharves when a fruit steamer is docking and pick out a stevedore who is less polite than his fellows. Take him uptown and teach him how to put studs into a dress shirt and station him at the entrance to your club. Tell him that he has just been unanimously chosen governor of the State

The choice of a head waiter is very important.

of New York and that it is up to him to maintain the prestige of the office. Also tell him that any patron is a bum until he proves himself otherwise. Show him what you mean by proof and then put it back into the cash drawer.

The interior of your club need cause you no worry —or expense. Hang some old awnings from the ceiling—good and low so as to shut off the air—and paint the walls red and yellow, with perhaps a figure or two in Russian costume, if you can draw—or even if you can't. In the center of the room build a dance floor just big enough for a medium-sized man to lie down on and roll over three times. Not that any medium-sized man is going to do it, but those are the standard measurements for night club dance floors. Fill the rest of the room with small tables which wabble, erect a platform for your jazz band, and you are set.

Now comes your big problem—the entertainment. There was a time when the patrons were satisfied to mill around on the dance floor and bump each other's hips. Then some foolish proprietor started in giving them a little show in between dances and they got spoiled. Now they all want a show for their money. This injustice to proprietors is somewhat mitigated by the fact that the patrons don't care what kind of show it is, so long as they don't have to dance.

There has to be some sort of master of ceremonies, and the proprietor can save a salary right there by doing this himself. All that he has to do is wear a dinner coat and act as if he believes that he has a good line.

"Ladies and gentlemen—and Gentiles. I have the very great honor to present to you tonight two of America's foremost ballroom dancers, two very charming and very talented young people who are filling an engagement at this club before beginning in the new Ziegfeld 'Follies.' They come fresh from a very successful season on the Riviera and I am sure that you will find them very, very delightful. So's your old man! . . . Come on, now, give these charming young people a good hand! . . . [*Lead the applause.*] Delacroix and Feeney, ladies and gentlemen!"

For Delacroix and Feeney it will be necessary to procure a young man and a young woman named Hyman and Gatz, respectively, who can waltz holding each other at arm's length. The young man must look at the young lady while they are waltzing and smile as if he really liked her, and the young lady must smile modestly back at him, just as if she were not thinking: "You big bum, I hope you trip and fall and break your shirt front." At the end of the waltz she curtsies so low that she has a good chance of not getting up again—which would be small loss. The master of ceremonies should then lead the applause again, what there is.

The entertainment over, you can turn the patrons loose again, with instructions to the orchestra to play so long that the dancers will fall exhausted by their tables and have to order refreshments. For food a forty-cent chop suey can be served for two dollars and a half and a ten-cent lemonade for a dollar. This will help you to clear expenses and maybe make a little profit.

Now in the matter of dispensing alcoholic drinks a great deal of caution must be used. It is, as many of you know, against the law to sell liquor, a fact which complicates its sale and makes for considerable inconvenience. The authorities are more and more on the alert and consequently the risk of getting caught remains about the same. A night club proprietor cannot be too careful to whom he sells strong drinks. For instance, if a man in the uniform of chief of police, with gold braid and a sword, comes in with a friend who has a flag in his hand on which is written "U. S. Revenue Service," no drinks should be served to that table until it has been definitely ascertained that the men are "all right." As for regular patrons, always wait until they ask for liquor before serving it, as a lot of people have their own with them and don't like to be bothered by representatives of the house standing at their elbows every minute trying to get them to buy. The chief thing to find out about a man before you sell him any illicit beverage is whether or not he has got $12. Once this is made sure, the thing is not so foolhardy.

With these few suggestions to those of you who might be in a position to start a night club, it is to be hoped that more and more citizens will lend a hand to help solve New York's big problem.

THE NEW VILLAINY

A LTHOUGH the new fall season in the drama is only just under way, it is not too early to view with alarm. Some Viewers-with-Alarm begin as early as September to view, but that doesn't give you much time to collect data. Perhaps all that you can get is a *datum*, but a good, healthy datum is enough to base a sizable alarm-view on, and, as you go along, you can make up a datum or two, so that you can refer to the whole as data.

This month we are chiefly worried about the status (or stata) of what used to be known as "the old-time religion." That is, its status in the world of drama. If the new season keeps on as the past two seasons have gone, being under suspicion of harboring religious thoughts will place one in the psychopathic class. For two years now, eight out of ten villains have been preachers and any layman with excessive religious tendencies has turned out to be just a repressed old sex-addict.

There was a time when the entrance of the preachers on the stage was the signal for a sigh of relief to go up, for you knew that so long as he stuck around, things were pretty sure to go as they should.

The lowest he ever reached in the dramatic scale
was when he was occasionally used for comedy
purposes. Once in a while there was a comic bishop,
but that was only natural. And any member of the
cast who showed signs of quoting the Scriptures, or
going to church, was pretty certain to be one of
those whom you could trust to help foil the adven-
turess in the last act.

Then along about the time that "Rain" settled
down for a run, we began to find preachers sneaking
into plays whose minds were not on their work in
the vineyard. Under the guise of evangelism they
started in to cut up. At first we thought: "Oh,
well, this is just an exception. Our Dr. Murnie at
home wouldn't do anything like this." But gradually, after we had seen dozens and dozens of
preachers come on in the first act, make a few sanc-
timonious remarks, and then sprout little horns and
a goat's tail, we began to look askance at even Dr.
Murnie of the Second Congregational Church.

Then the lay members of the congregation came
in for analysis. The hand of Freud reached out and
touched the brethren and sistren and we learned that
whenever anyone is excessively religious, it is a sign
that they are suffering from an inhibition which is
likely some day to break loose and leave Broadway
strewn with bits of broken bottles and confetti. The

If you were highly strung you whispered out loud to the
heroine.

more religious they are, the more they crave a good, rip-snorting week-end at Atlantic City, registering under the wrong name. It is all very confusing.

In the old days, the minute a man came on with a mustache like Adolphe Menjou's and wearing a pair of riding boots with a crop to slap them with, you could be pretty sure that he was up to no good. If you were highly strung you whispered out loud to the heroine not to go to the city with him as he had no more intention of marrying her than—well, than anything at all, and you know how little that is.

Today, whenever a character in clerical cloth makes his entrance, the orchestra starts picking at the violin strings in the old *pizzicato* villain-entrance music, the young-lady members of the cast pick their exits and the audience settles back in preparation for the dirty work.

Pretty soon we may have a scene like this:

SCENE.—*Living room of the DeViblis home. Father, mother, and daughter are seated around the table, splicing rope.*

DAUGHTER: Pa, there's somethin' I been a-wantin' to ask you fer a long time.

MOTHER: For heaven's sake, daughter, talk straight. This isn't a New England farm play we're in. You know how to talk better than that.

DAUGHTER: Well, anyway, I want to marry Arthur Arthritis.

FATHER: What does he do for a living?

DAUGHTER: Well, he's changing his job in a few months.

FATHER: What does he do now?

DAUGHTER: Why—er—well, I'll tell you; just now he's a preacher, but he's going to change—

MOTHER: A preacher! Oh, my!

FATHER: A minister of the gospel? Where did you meet him? I thought I told you not to run around with them religious folks. They are every one of them inhibited.

DAUGHTER: Oh, that's just because you don't know them, dad. They're just as decent as you or I when you get to know them. And Arthur isn't *really* a preacher. He's just filling-in.

FATHER: Just filling-in, eh? I suppose you know what that leads to? Next he'll be having a little parish of his own, then he'll get a call to a big city, or perhaps he'll even sink so low as to be a missionary. Them preachers are all missionaries at heart, and you know what missionaries are. No, sir, no daughter of mine gets mixed up in that crowd.

DAUGHTER: Well, he's coming here in a few minutes to hear your answer. There he is now!

(*Enter the Rev. Heemerson.*)

FATHER: Well, what do you want here?

THE REV. H.: Why, Brother—

FATHER: Don't you "brother" me.

THE REV. H.: I love your daughter and I want to marry her.

FATHER: You want to *marry* her, eh? When you get to New York, I suppose?

THE REV. H.: Why, I thought—

FATHER (*stepping to the telephone*): Oh, you thought, did you? (*To central*): Give me police headquarters . . . hello, police headquarters? Well, there's a preacher in my house. Send an officer up right away!

THE REV. H. (*leaving*): I'm sorry, sir, that you feel this way, so I think I'll be saying "good-by."

FATHER: Good-by, and go back to your religious crowd and their loose ways and never darken my door again.

(*Curtain with daughter crying, and father and mother getting down the family volume of Freud to read by the lamplight.*)

.   .   .   .

All this is perhaps the result of years and years of bullyragging the stage and stage folk by preachers and religious zealots. The stage folk have found a comeback and are using it. It will be nip and tuck for a while, with the stage folk slightly in the lead until it is discovered that all stage folk are not really saints and all religious zealots not really satyrs and nymphs. Then things will settle down again. In the meantime, let's have some more of that chicken potpie, please.

TIME-OFF FROM THE SHOW

New York Sights Which the Visitor Should Not Miss

YOU can't expect the visitor to New York during the automobile show to stand in front of automobiles all day and all night. He's got to look at something else *once* in a while, just so that he can see the automobiles better when he goes back to look at them. That's only common sense.

Now comes the big question—what to look at? New York is a big city now, and unless you are careful you will look at the wrong things and before you know it, it will be time to go back and you will have seen nothing. Or practically nothing. Or next to nothing.

Let us say (Oh, go on! Be a good sport! *Let* us), let us say that you are to be in New York four days and six nights. Here is a schedule which you may follow or not, but, at any rate, look it over. It suggests something for you to do every evening and, in case you have any spare time during the day, there are one or two extra hints.

MONDAY EVENING

Of course, the very first night that you have free you will want to see the new Reinach collection of tapestries at the Metropolitan Art Museum. This collection is one of the most valuable in the world, and one of the hardest to hide under. The tapestries hang some four feet off the ground, so the minute you try to hide under one of them you are quite exposed up to at least your chest, maybe oftener than that.

Most of the tapestries in the exhibit are French, and consequently are kept in a little room off the main hall, to which admission is obtained only by conference with the curator. Of the others, the most interesting is that which depicts the hunting of a stag in the Middle Ages. In the lower left-hand corner you see the huntsmen starting out after the stag, carrying hauberks and falcons. As you work up through the tapestry, from left to right, it gets even less interesting, until, by the time they have caught the stag in the upper right-hand corner, you aren't looking at it at all and have passed on to the next tapestry which shows huntsmen of the Middle Ages chasing a fox.

It has just occurred to us that the Art Museum is not open evenings; so this plan for Monday night

is out. You will have to find something else to do.
There is a good place on West Fifty-sixth Street.

TUESDAY EVENING

The Public Library, at Forty-second Street and
Fifth Avenue, is open until 11 o'clock. You will
surely want to see this. Enter by the side door on
the Forty-second Street side, as there are two of the
nastiest lions you ever saw guarding the front entrance. Ring the little bell by the side entrance and
when the man comes ask for Joe Delaney. He will
ask who wants to see him and you say that Bob
Benchley sent you. He will then let you in to the
downstairs lobby, where there is an elevator to take
you up to the reading room. This elevator is not
running; so you will have to walk up three flights of
marble stairs, and a pretty tough pull it is, too.

You will find the reading room brilliantly lighted
and practically full of books. Go straight to the
case marked "Biography M-TO." Beginning at the
top shelf, left-hand corner, pull all the books out,
from left to right, and throw them in a pile on the
floor. Pretty soon you will have quite a big pile
and can begin on the case marked "History-Renais-
sance." This will make another big pile. By this
time, you will have several attendants helping you

and you can work faster. If you stick to it until 11 o'clock, you will be able to pull out all the books on that side of the room and scuffle through them. Then you can go back to your hotel, tired but happy.

WEDNESDAY EVENING

By this time, you will be perhaps ready to see a little of the so-called "night life" of the metropolis. There is no better place to do this than at the Woman's Exchange, on Madison Avenue between Fifty-fourth and Fifty-fifth Streets. The specialty here is breads and cakes, and if you can get a table by the window you can eat your fill while watching the Madison Avenue trolley cars go thundering by. It would be well to wear your old clothes to this place, as along about 9 o'clock in the evening things begin to rough up quite a bit, and, by the time the fresh batch of cup cakes is ready at 10, the joint is a regular bedlam. It was here that Harry Thaw had been dining the night he shot Stanford White.

THURSDAY EVENING

We have saved until your last night in New York the big thrill of the week—riding on the Shetland ponies in Central Park. They usually put the ponies

About nine o'clock things begin to rough up quite a bit.

to bed at sundown, but by slipping the pony-man a dollar bill you can get him to leave as many of the little fellows out as you may require.

Get to the park at about 8 p. m., wearing red coat and riding breeches. You might as well take along a good, big whip, too, in case your pony gets fresh. Carrying children about all day as they do, they are quite apt to think that they can do anything they like, and you must be ready to show them that they can't. They will respect you all the more after a couple of good belts.

Once aboard the ponies, the best course is around the reservoir. Five times around at a brisk canter makes a nice ride. In case your feet drag on the ground (the ponies are pretty small) you can tuck them in under the saddle or else let them drag. For steeplechase racing it will be better to let them drag, as it makes it harder for the little animals to get over the hurdles. If you have lots of money to spend on the thing, you can give a hunt breakfast at the Central Park Casino.

ALTERNATE ENTERTAINMENT

Although you may have seen something of the automobile at the show, you will get a better idea of what the automobile really means to our civilization by coming with me to a little private exhibition which I will be glad to stage any afternoon between the hours of 4 and 6:30. I wish that every automobile manufacturer and salesman could join in, because I want them to see just what it is that they have done. If I had my way, I would get them all reservations on a train leaving the Pennsylvania station at 5:30 p. m. Then, at 4:45, I would start them from Forty-fourth Street in taxicabs or private cars and say: "Now, you big automobile men you have got forty-five minutes to go half a mile in. And there isn't another train until tomorrow morning."

I would follow behind on foot, and when they were held up by the jam of automobiles at Forty-second Street for five minutes, I would jeer. When they were held up at Fortieth Street, I would hoot. During their five-minute holdup at Thirty-ninth Street, I would taunt them with: "What price automobiles, now?" and while they were chafing at the tieup at Thirty-eighth Street, I would call out: "Get a horse!" I would make them so sore at the automobile as an institution that they would swear never to make another.

THE *LIFE* POLAR EXPEDITION

*C*ONTINUATION *of the log of Bobby Benchley, Juvenile Yoeman on* LIFE'S *North Pole
Expedition.*

MT. KISCO, N. Y.—*En route to North Pole by
bicycle.*

Things have been going from bad to worse in this
expedition and I doubt very much if I can stick it
out any longer. My father has been unbearable
ever since we left North White Plains, harping con-
tinually on the fact that I am only seven years old
and small for my age at that. If parents only knew
it, it is that sort of talk which makes for radicalism
and debauchery in the younger generation.

Then he began insisting that I mention the names
of firms which have contributed stuff for our expedition. When I say that we stopped at the road-side
for lunch I must add "which was so kindly contributed by the Alexander Hamilton Peanut Butter
Sandwich Co., of 1145 North Rumsey Street, Chicago." Or if I mention tipping our hats to a lady,
acknowledgment must be given to the "Bon Ton

Arctic Hat Co., who were generous enough to supply the expedition with hats."

Now this is a lot of hooey and I told my father so and refused point-blank to lend myself to any such cheap advertising gag as that. It was then that he brought up the point that I was only seven and that I should busy myself with only those thoughts which a seven-year-old boy should have. And he added, furthermore, that I could keep a civil tongue in my head. So I have determined to stop off here at Mt. Kisco and spend a week or so with the Barry kids and then go on back home to Scarsdale. That expedition is never going to get to the North Pole anyway. My father and Lieut.-Commander Connelly are too fat—especially my father. You ought to see him.

Insert in log made by Benchley, Sr.

Bobby has proved quite a disappointment to us so far, and I am not sure that I would be sorry to see him leave the expedition here. Our idea in having him along was to give the boy a little publicity and to have him write a book which could be sold to the juvenile trade around Christmas time, but a little boy who behaves as badly as he does doesn't deserve any publicity and he can't write for a darn anyway.

Furthermore, I am *not* getting fat.   I always put on a little weight in the winter, because I can't play tennis, but every one says that it is becoming to me. I weigh only 160 when I am ready for my cold-bath (which I very seldom am, *these* mornings) and for a man of my height, that is not a pound too much. As a matter of fact, Bobby is probably a little sore because he is so small for his age.   You'd never think he was seven.   He looks more like a child of three.   He must get that from his mother's side of the family, because all the Benchleys have shot right up to a good height before they were seven.   His older brother Nat is a fine tall boy.   And a great deal smarter in school than Bobby.

Then, too, another sign that I am not too fat is that people who haven't seen me for several years all remark "How well you look!"   You don't say that to a man who is *too* fat, do you?

But there is no reason for having our expedition torn with dissension just because a little boy has no respect for his father.   I suggested sending him back to Scarsdale, but Lieut.-Commander Connelly said why not give him another chance, he is so cute. It is all very well for an outsider to call a child cute, but when a man has reached my age he is entitled to a little respect from his own children— it seems to me.

(Resumption of the log by Bobby.)

It is very nice here in Mt. Kisco at the Barrys' and I wouldn't be surprised if the whole expedition stayed here until the snow gets out of the roads. Mr. Barry has some very good stuff that he brought from France last year and I heard my father say last night that he wouldn't care if he *never* saw the North Pole or anything else for that matter. He and Lieut.-Commander Connelly think they are pretty good at two-part singing and as Lieut.-Commander Connelly said, "It looks as if it were going to be a fine winter for two-part singing, especially 'Sleep, Kentucky Babe.'" Mr. Barry hasn't said anything yet except that he has to take his family to Cannes early in March. All he expected us to do was stop here overnight, and while he is very nice about it, I guess he knows what he is in for, all right all right.

On the way up from North White Plains I saw a snow-bird, but didn't say anything about it as I knew it would mean taking out pencils and making notes for the Museum. A hot lot of good the Museum is going to get out of *this* expedition.

SPYING ON THE VEHICULAR TUNNEL

BEFORE the formal opening of the Holland Vehicular Tunnel under the Hudson River, it behooves New Yorkers to study up a little on the subject and see why it is that 46,000 vehicles are going to *want* to go to Jersey City every day.

In order to present this problem fairly to the readers of this paper, the writer of this article (you must guess) took a tour of inspection of the tube, which is now completed with the exception of installing a ventilation system and hanging the curtains. Curtains make such a difference that it will probably be simply another tunnel when they are up.

Your investigator was not asked by the authorities to make this tour of inspection, but somebody from the New York *Times* went through the thing and wrote a story about it; so there didn't seem to be any good reason why a reporter from *The New Yorker* shouldn't. Not having the permission of the tunnel authorities, he went alone into this vast-two-mile submarine passageway, with the result that he got lost and is still in there. This story is being sent out to *The New Yorker* by a code of tappings executed on the roof of the giant shell by the lost investigator. As soon as he finishes sending in copy (which will be relayed to the publication offices by a special tugboat and automobile service) the reporter will turn his energies again to the problem of getting out of the tube. After all, there are only two ways possible in which to go; so it ought not to be very difficult. The big problem comes in trying to decide which way to take.

Now that we are well acquainted it might be less formal if I use the first person. You probably knew that it was I all along anyway. These little editorial subterfuges are rather futile.

But to get back to the tunnel—or rather to get *out* of the tunnel. Sneaking in by the entrance at Canal Street, Manhattan, I made my way through the tiled passageway for what must have been a mile before I realized that, really, when you have seen the first hundred feet of a vehicular tunnel you have seen all 9250. I had got the idea by then. The next problem was whether to go on ahead to the Jersey City exit or turn and go back to Canal Street. Not knowing how far I had come, I couldn't figure out which way would be the shorter. Then, in turning around several times to see if I could make out any light at either end, I forgot which was the way to New York and which the way to Jersey City. This was quite terrifying and I began to cry softly. I

I attracted the attention of a passing tug.

made frantic little starts, first in one direction and then in the other, and finally sat down on the ground and sobbed myself to sleep.

When I awoke, it was high time that my story was in; so I attracted the attention of a passing tug by tapping on the roof of the tube and indicated that I had a story to file for *The New Yorker*. The rest is history.

Well, anyway.

The Holland Vehicular Tunnel is a dandy tunnel, all right, all right. The roadways are 20 feet wide and there is 13 feet, 6 inches of headroom. The extra six inches is for wedding parties in which there are men in silk hats. It is estimated that in one year 15,000,000 vehicles will pass through the tube. Wouldn't you like to have a dollar for every vehicle! A dollar and a *half* would be even better. *Boy!* What I couldn't do with $22,500,000!

I was pleased to note that there are to be telephone stations along the route. This will make it possible to call up and say:

"Look here! I'm held up in the vehicular tunnel and probably can't get anything before the 8:15. Don't wait dinner. I'll eat in Jersey City."

This question of being held up in the tunnel is one which must present itself to everyone who gives the matter any thought at all. There aren't many things certain in this life, but there is one event I can predict without even adding "maybe." On my first trip through the vehicular tunnel at the wheel of my high-powered car, just as I get halfway between New York and New Jersey, with a line of impatient Sunday automobilists behind me, I am going to run out of gas. I'll bet that the engineers in charge have never once thought of this contingency, and when it arises, it is going to make their tunnel look pretty silly. It was a silly idea anyway in the first place.

COMPILING AN AMERICAN TRAGEDY

*Suggestions as to How Theodore Dreiser Might
Write His Next Human Document and
Save Five Years' Work*

CHAPTER I

UP East Division Street, on a hot day in late
July, walked two men, one five feet four, the
other, the taller of the two, five feet six, the first
being two inches shorter than his more elongated
companion, and consequently giving the appearance
to passers-by on East Division Street, or, whenever the two reached a cross-street, to the passers-
by on the cross-street, of being at least a good two
inches shorter than the taller of the little group.

Walking up East Division Street they came, in
two or three minutes, to Division Street proper,
which runs at right angles and a little to the left
of East Division Street, but not so much to the left
as Marcellus Street, or Ransome Street, for that
matter. As the two continued strolling, in that
fashion in which two men of their respective heights
are likely to stroll, they came in succession to—

(NOTE TO PRINTER: *Attached find copy of Thurston's Street Guide. Print names of every street listed therein, beginning with East Division and up to, and including, Dawson.*)

CHAPTER II

That these two men, presented in the last chapter, would eventually stop walking up Division Street and enter a house of some sort or description, might well be anticipated by the reader, and, in fact, such was the case.

It was, indeed, the house of the shorter of the two, of the one whom we have seen in the last chapter to have been five feet four, if, indeed, he was. It was a typical dwelling, or home, of a man of the middle-class in a medium-sized city such as the one in which these men found themselves living.

(NOTE TO PRINTER: *Attached find insurance inventory of household effects and architect's specifications. Reproduce in toto.*)

CHAPTER III

Reaching the living-room described above, Tom Rettle, for such was the name of the shorter of the two—the one to whom the house, or home, or dwelling, belonged—was greeted by his wife, Anna, a buxom woman of perhaps thirty-four or thirty-five, certainly not *more* than thirty-five, if one were to judge by her fresh, wholesome color and the sparkle of her brownish-gray eyes, or even by her well-rounded form, her—

(*Print attached passport description of Anna Rettle.*)

"Well, hello, Anna," said Tom, pleasantly, for Tom Rettle was, as a matter of fact, a very pleasant man unless he were angered, and his blue eyes smiled in a highly agreeable manner.

"Well, hello, Tom," replied Anna, for it was indeed Anna who spoke, in a soft, well-modulated voice, too, giving the impression of being an extremely agreeable sort of a woman.

"Anna, I want you to meet a very good friend of mine, Arthur Berolston, a very good friend of mine," said Tom, politely, looking, at the same time, at both Anna and Berolston.

"I'm very happy to meet Mr. Berolston," added Anna, genially, although one could see that in her heart she wished that Tom would bring a little different type of friends home, a thing she had often spoken to him about when they were alone, as they often were.

"Dat's very good of yer ter say, Missus Rettle," replied Berolston, in modern slang, which made him sound even more uncouth than he looked, which was uncouth enough. "For de love o' Mike!"

At this indication of a rough bringing-up on the part of her husband's acquaintance, Anna Rettle winced slightly but showed no other sign of her emotions. Tom was such a kind-hearted fellow! So good! So kind-hearted! Tom was.

"What is there for supper tonight, Anna?" asked Tom, when the wincing had died down. "You know how well I like cole slaw, and have always liked it."

"I certainly do know your fondness for cole slaw, Tom," replied his wife, but with a note of regret in her voice, for she was thinking that she had no cole slaw for supper on the particular night of which we are speaking. "But you will remember that we had cole slaw last night with the cold tongue, and night before last with the baked beans and—"

(*Run attached "Fifteen Midsummer Menus for Cole Slaw Lovers."*)

CHAPTER IV

Prepared as Tom was not to have cole slaw for supper, he could not hide his disappointment. Anna had been a good wife to him.

But somehow tonight, when he had brought Arthur Berolston home to supper, his disappointment was particularly keen, for he and Arthur had been discussing cole slaw all the way up East Division Street, across Division Street and through to the southwest corner of Dawson and Margate, where Tom lived, and each had said how much he liked it.

Should he strike Anna for failing him at this juncture? He, Tom Rettle, strike his wife, Anna Rettle? And, even if he should decide to strike her, *where* should he direct the blow? Tom's mind was confused with all these questions.

(*Reprint the above paragraph twenty-five times.*)

CHAPTERS V-LXXXII INCLUSIVE

To PRINTER: *With the above copy you will find a brief-case containing newspaper clippings giving the complete testimony of Anna Rettle, Thomas Rettle and Arthur Berolston in the case of "ANNA RETTLE VS. THOMAS RETTLE," tried in the Criminal Court of Testiman County, September 2-28, 1925. There is also a transcript of the testimony of three neighbors of the Rettles' (Herman Nordquist, Ethel Nordquist and Junior Nordquist), and of Officer Louis M. Hertzog of the Fifth Precinct. Reprint all these and, at the bottom of the last page, put "THE END."*

STORM WARNINGS FOR NEW YORK

ANYONE wishing to see New York summer shows, or any other New York shows for that matter, had better run like everything. Any day now the walls of th city are going to topple in, and, with a blare of trumpets, the Forces of the Lord are going to smite New York, even as Sodom and Gomorrah were smitten. New York is riding for its Big Fall, and it wouldn't be surprising if it came around the end of this week.

Probably never before in the history of disrobing (see Taine's "A Short History of Unhooking and Unbuttoning," Harpers', 1897, 1 vol., 345-pp. octavo) have so many young ladies appeared with so few clothes before so many people at once. It is recorded that in ancient Rome the *puellæ* wore fewer clothes at the annual outings, but their audiences were comparatively small and selected from a list of socially possible people. Today, in the Borough of Manhattan, the young folks appear before a Winter Garden full of practical strangers—that is, they are strangers at the beginning of the show. By the end of the first act, it is as if they had known them all their lives. Just as no man is a stranger (or a hero) to his Swedish rubber, so, by the price of a ticket to "The Great Temptations" you can have at least twenty people in New York whom you know awfully, awfully well. And yet they say that New York is cold and aloof!

All this levity on my part is just whistling past the graveyard. I, personally, am pretty worried. You can push the Forces of Vengea ce just so far and then—buckety-buckety—down comes the ceiling. Ask the Sodom Chamber of Commerce. And the worst of it is, that just as the rain sheds its benefits on the just and the unjust alike, the fact that you have been home and in bed every nigh : at ten o'clock isn't going to help you a bit when your whole city begins to smell as if something was burning and then suddenly goes up in a puff of brimstone. You can't go out and argue with a Pillar of Fire and explain that you, personally, have been spending your evenings building bookcases. If your town goes, you go too, and no back-talk.

Now, in my case, the prospects are even more depressing, because the job from which I eke out barely enough money to buy gin for my children makes it necessary that I attend the opening performances of all these wrath-provoking shows. I don't like them. I would never go to see them if it were not for the fact that it is my life-work. Often I sit

I *am* unquestionably on record as sitting in D-113.

through them with my eyes shut. But I *am* unquestionably on record in the office of the Snooping Angel as sitting in D-113 at the Winter Garden. And when they are making out their lists for culprits to be hit on the head by falling walls or swirled up into the skies on a fiery horse with nine heads, my name probably is right there among the "B's" as a constant and incorrigible attendant at these festivals of sin. The angel probably doesn't do more than take a look over the audience. You can't expect him to go to the box-office and see who paid to get in or find out why they are there.

If I get through this summer all right, I am going to hire an assistant. Then, whenever a Shubert show is announced or something called "A Nuit in Paree," I will slip him the seats and say: "Here, Joe, go and enjoy yourself." In this way I may be able to escape the extra heavy punishment in store for participants and get out of the general cataclysm with perhaps just a broken ankle or singed eyelashes. It is going to be bad enough for the simple bystanders without getting mixed up in the private showing. The only break that I have ever had in this line was that I was in France at the time of Earl Carroll's champagne-bath party in New York. When I got back I found my invitation on my desk. If I *had* been there, covering the affair for my paper, they would have taken flashlight photographs.

And, after all, what fun is there in going to these displays? "The Great Temptations," for example, probably contains fewer real temptations than a Christian Endeavor convention. The thing is too unreal ever to constitute actual menace. You hear somebody announcing that, if the audience will remain seated, there will now be a parade showing the way parsnips are cooked in all the different countries of the world. Then eight girls walk across the stage, one representing Nell Gwyn cooking parsnips, one Cleopatra, one Thaïs, and so forth. It is very dull indeed, and the fact that the girls are clad as if they were just getting ready to turn on the hot water doesn't help, or hurt, anything. The whole thing is highly academic, and unless you are interested in the cooking of parsnips, you are going to find yourself looking at your program to see how long it will take to empty the theater with every seat filled. If the Forces of Judgment only knew it, the display of what the advertisements call "feminine pulchritude" is one of the most innocuous of all forms of theatrical entertainment. It is like looking in at a delicatessen window. It is too much.

However, try to tell that to the Watch and Ward Society. Try to convince that great, big old Nine-

Headed Horse, when he comes snorting down out of a cloud of fire with a flaming subpœna made out in your name, that these exhibitions bore you. Just say to him, if you can make your voice heard above the thunder and lightning and bellowing rocks, that a show where a nine-tenths naked lady walks across the stage means no more to you than watching the Stamford local go through New Rochelle, and listen to him laugh. Why, you will probably get a million years extra in the biscuit oven just for saying such a thing.

You see, he has heard that line a good many times and he is getting a little tired of it, just as you would, yourself, after the first few million years. He knows that nobody ever will admit that he goes where he shouldn't because he likes it. Every single time it is a case of being on duty, as you might say; making an investigation for some reform agency, or getting material for a book, or showing an out-of-town customer a good time. Even the out-of-town customer has the alibi that he is just trying to find out whether things are really as bad in New York as the papers have been saying they are. He would much rather have spent the evening writing a report to the firm about conditions in the textile industry, but he didn't think that he could afford to miss an opportunity to get some first-hand information about the decadence of the present age.

So the only thing that there is left to do, if we are going to save ourselves and the biggest city in the country from a horrible fate, is to stop the Messrs. Shubert from putting on shows like that. And the way to stop them from putting on shows like that is to go to them and say: "Messrs. Shubert, put down that mending for just a minute, I want to talk to you. I am a married man with a family and I have a lot of work that I have to do before I die. I have insurance to pay up and I have a house which has to be painted before it can be sold. Now, you and your shows are leading this whole city into inevitable destruction at the hands of the Forces of Vengeance. No city can go on as New York is going on giving pageants about the twelve different ways of cooking parsnips, without incurring Divine Wrath to a fatal extent. Won't you, for the sake of the wife and kiddies, put, let us say, a girdle of large hydrangeas on your choruses and perhaps an old-fashioned shawl? Won't you arrange it so that it won't be quite so incriminating for a man who wants to go straight to be numbered among the patrons of your entertainments?"

And if the Messrs. Shubert just laugh and go on with their mending or whatever it is that they hap-

pen to be doing at the time, the only thing left for
me to do, at any rate, is to do my duty without
flinching—accept my complimentary tickets, and go
to these shows wearing a tin helmet and carrying a
letter from my pastor in my pocket against the Day
of Judgment.

THE *LIFE* POLAR EXPEDITION

M T. KISCO, New York, January 21st.—At a meeting of the older members of the expedition last night it was voted to ask Bobby for his resignation, not in any spirit of anger but simply because it was felt that he wasn't in sympathy with the aims and policies of those in command. Lieut.-Commander Connelly was elected to inform Bobby and to see that he got his carfare back to Scarsdale.

Bobby had anticipated our action, however, by resigning on his own hook and was already on his way home with one of the Barry children in the Barrys' car, leaving a note to the effect that he was pretty tired of the whole thing and doubted whether the expedition would reach the Pole at all because of having so many fat men on it.

And so ends the first really unfortunate episode of our trip. As Bobby grows older he probably will acquire more repression and will learn that individual whims must sometimes give way to the common good. I also hope that he starts growing tall pretty soon.

With the discordant element out of the way, the next thing to do was to plan for our hop-off. We still have quite a distance to go before we even get in sight of the Pole and we must be moving. So a meeting was called in the Barrys' study, to which Mr. Barry was, *ex-officio,* invited, as it was thought that he might have some suggestions. His very first suggestion was excellent; it was, in part, to concoct an eggnog, a hot eggnog. He had some very good eggs, he said, and added that that was one of the advantages of living in the country—you get good eggs. This was voted on, and it was decided that Mr. Barry was right. So the eggnog was made hot and the meeting called to order.

Lieut.-Commander Connelly said that we ought to decide how we were to overcome the retarding action of deep snow on our wheels. We have made several trial spins around the house here, just to see that our cycles were in good order, and found (*a*) that they were not, and (*b*) that even if they had been, the snow would have made any kind of progress at all very difficult. As Lieut.-Commander Connelly said, "It is almost as if someone were actually holding the wheels back!"

From there the discussion got around to cases in which wheels actually *had* been held back by some unseen force, but nobody had ever heard of such cases. Ensign Thermaline said that he knew of a case once where a man with hypnotic power had put a friend under a spell and made it impossible for him to move his hand away from his face. Mr. Barry asked whose face it was the man's hand was on, his own or the hypnotizer's, and Ensign Thermaline said that he had never thought to inquire, but that he could get the man on the telephone in a jiffy and find out. We all said that it would be interesting to know. So a telephone book was sent for and Ensign Thermaline set about looking up his friend's number.

While this was going on, we got back to the business of the expedition and the question of when we should start on. Our route lies pretty fairly straight ahead of us, on up through Westchester County to Massachusetts, then on up through New Hampshire to Canada, and from there to the Pole. "It ought to be very pretty up around Williamstown at this time of year," said Lieut.-Commander Connelly. "That's where Williams College is." Everyone agreed to this and it was remembered that the Williams song, "The Royal Purple," has some very neat harmony to it. Furthermore, it was discovered that Mr. Barry sings a very passable baritone, and a baritone is the one thing that our expedition has lacked, for Lieut.-Commander Connelly twists out a very

tricky tenor, and with me leading and Ensign Thermaline on a low but fairly accurate bass it began
to look as if we might do something worth while
after all.

"Here's a funny thing," spoke up Ensign Thermaline, still buried in the telephone book. "There are
two people by the name of 'Gepp,' both living in
Jersey City. A 'Ben F. Gepp' at 218 Belvidere Ave.,
and a 'William A. Gepp' at 82 Jewett Ave."

"Probably brothers," suggested Mr. Barry.

"Not necessarily," retorted Lieut.-Commander
Connelly, a little testily.

"All right; cousins then," said Mr. Barry, and
the threatened hard-feeling was avoided. Mr. Barry
would be a very good man to have come along with
us to the Pole as he is very conciliatory and diplo-
matic, and after Bobby we need somebody like that.

As a matter of fact, I suggested to him that he
come with us and he said that he really ought to
take his family to Cannes in March as he had promised them. But he added that he was almost per-
suaded to give that plan up and come along with us.
I suggested that we go right then and sound out
Mrs. Barry on the subject because I was sure that
we could make her see the thing in the right light.
So we all went upstairs to look for Mrs. Barry, but
she was asleep. Lieut.-Commander Connelly sug-

gested a little serenade, on the ground that married women get little or no romance in their lives, and said that if he knew married women at all Mrs. Barry would be very glad to have a serenade sung outside her door, asleep or not. So we did "The Royal Purple" for her, very soft the first time through and then crescendo on the repeat.

Then, at Mrs. Barry's suggestion, we went to bed.